The Lost Art
of Intercession

Restoring the Power and Passion
of the Watch of the Lord

The Lost Art of Intercession

**Restoring the Power and Passion
of the Watch of the Lord**

Jim W. Goll

Watch of the Lord™ is a registered trademark of Mahesh Chavda Ministries International, All Nations Church, Charlotte, North Carolina.

Take note that the name satan and related names are not capitalized. We choose not to acknowledge him, even to the point of violating grammatical rules.

Revival Press
An Imprint of
Destiny Image® Publishers, Inc.
P.O. Box 310
Shippensburg, PA 17257-0310

ISBN 1-56043-697-2

For Worldwide Distribution
Printed in the U.S.A.

This book and all other Destiny Image, Revival Press
and Treasure House books are available
at Christian bookstores and distributors worldwide.

For a U.S. bookstore nearest you, call **1-800-722-6774**.
For more information on foreign distributors, call **717-532-3040**.
Or reach us on the Internet: **http://www.reapernet.com**

Visit the author's website at **http://www.reapernet.com/mttn**

Acknowledgment

Over the years, I have had the high privilege of being impacted by some of the greatest teachers and generals of prayer. Their deposits into my life have been rich and irreplaceable. But, it is to the "little butlers" that I owe the most thanks to. I thank the Lord for all those sacrificial servants who have helped to hold up my arms as we continue with endurance to run the race that is set before us.

I have also had the blessing of a family who has released and blessed me to be all that I can be in God, to be the unique vessel God has created me to be. I want to thank my family—especially my parents, Wayne and Amanda Goll—for all your support. Thanks, mom, for marking my life with the spirit of prayer for our King.

Endorsements

"Authority and power reside in this book because it comes out of a life that has 'done,' and then taught. Finally, these precious, forged gems are out before us. Feast your eyes and let these truths change your life! Get ready to take a ride into new dimensions of intercession and worship in your personal and corporate prayer life." —**Wesley Tullis, Director, The Jericho Center for Prayer and World Evangelization, Colorado Springs, Colorado**

"Jim Goll is one of the most passionate, intercessory-prophetic persons, regarding the things of God, whom I have met. His teachings have been very helpful to me and I know they will be very enriching to those who read this book." —**Randy Clark, Senior Pastor, St. Louis Vineyard Christian Fellowship, Global Awakening Team Leader, St. Louis, Missouri**

"If you want to be consumed on the altar of God, if you want your heart to be enlarged for God's full purposes in our generation, then you will profit from this book. The Psalmist says that God confides in those who fear Him. The Lord confides different things to different people so that we need each other to become whole. Jim Goll fears the Lord and the Lord has confided some things to him that I needed. You need them too." —**Dr. Don Finto, Pastor, Belmont Family of Churches, Nashville, Tennessee**

"Jim Goll has had a significant impact on my life personally and on that of Harvest Rock Church. He's a man who hears from God and has the character to obey accordingly. I highly commend what he has to say about the urgency and art of intercession in this crucial hour." —**Che Ahn, D. Min., Senior Pastor, Harvest Rock Church; Founder of Harvest International Ministries, Pasedena, California**

"I have known Jim Goll for more than 15 years, and I appreciate his passion for Jesus and gifting in intercession and the prophetic. Jim was the Director of the School of the Spirit at our Grace Training Center in Kansas City for six years, and his classes were among the favorites of our students." —**Mike Bickle, Senior Pastor, Metro Christian Fellowship, Kansas City, Missouri; Author,** *Passion for Jesus.*

"Enough cannot be said for Jim Goll's latest addition to the arsenal of profound yet practical books on prayer. *The Lost Art of Intercession* is not some dry, academic treatise on prayer. No! It pulsates with prophetic life, complete with angelic visitations, visions, and miracles. It's just plain exciting stuff! Also, knowing both Jim and Michal Ann as I do, these stories are not merely the secondhand recitation of other people's experiences, but rather firsthand visitations like those in Bible days. I've heard many people speak and teach on prayer, but Jim Goll is one of the best yet. Don't let this book get by you." —**Wesley Campbell, Author,** *Welcoming a Visitation of the Holy Spirit,* **Producer of the "Praying the Bible" Series**

" 'We are epistles written and read of all men.' What makes this book credible is not only its insight into the ministry of intercession, but also the author. Jim is no novice—he is a seasoned warrior. His writings are not the gleanings of a researcher; rather they are the lessons gained in the trenches of experience. Jim lives the life of an intercessor—read and follow his example." — **David Ravenhill, Pastor, The Vineyard of Gig Harbor, Gig Harbor, Washington; Author,** *For God's Sake, Grow Up!*

Contents

Foreword

In January of 1995 the Lord said to us, **"Watch with Me."** In response we invited about 20 people to spend from 10:00 p.m. Friday till 6:00 a.m. Saturday keeping the "night watch," which is going without sleep for spiritual reasons. We waited on God in worship and prayer and shared in communion through Jesus' Body and Blood in the Lord's Supper. Every Friday night since we have done the same. We have celebrated the Watch with as many as 4,000 watchmen present. Watch groups are now springing up here and abroad. We find ourselves in the midst of a renewed visitation that is manifesting the glory of the Lord!

Prayer is the backbone of the Church. God is restoring our spiritual genetics as we keep the Watch. We are experiencing a new dimension of communion with the Lord. He is redefining our understanding of prayer.

The Lord is speaking a new word about an old word. The old word is **"Pray!"** The new word is **"Pray corporately!"** The Lord is opening our eyes to this simple truth: *Prayer is where everything begins and ends in the realm of the spirit.* It is where everything is accomplished. Prayer is the true genetic code of the Church. We have experienced other mutant genes that have caused us to evolve away from God's true design for His Body. *But nothing God is going to do will happen without prayer.*

Watching is a historical part of every great ministry and every great revival. An excerpt from John Wesley's journal of 1739 reads,

"Mr. Hall, Kitchen, Ingram, Whitfield, Hutchings, and my brother Charles were present at our love feast at Fetter Lane with about sixty of our brethren. At about 3:00 in the morning as we were continuing instant in prayer, the power of God came upon us so much that many cried out for exceeding joy and many fell to the ground. As soon as we recovered a little from the awe and amazement of his majesty, we broke out with one voice, 'We praise Thee, oh God! We acknowledge Thee to be the Lord!' "

Joel and the people of Israel, Wesley, the Moravians, and other groups have pioneered in all night prayer. They tilled the ground and planted the seeds of God's heart for corporate prayer. God is now watering the seeds of revival and raising up watchmen to reap a new harvest through prayer.

One of these watchmen the Lord has been raising up is Jim Goll. It has been Bonnie's and my privilege to be intimately involved in the lives of Jim and Michal Ann Goll for several years. We love their passionate hunger for seeing a generation of prayer warriors arise.

In February of 1996 at a conference where we both ministered, I sent forth a call for "watchmen to take their stand on the wall." One of the first in line was, of course, my dear friend, Jim Goll. As he stood before me as a soldier waiting for his next orders, the Holy Spirit rose up inside me and I released a proclamation, "You are called as a General in the Watch of the Lord!" Little did I know at the time that Jim would be used to write this needed book on *The Lost Art of Intercession: Restoring the Power and Passion of the Watch of the Lord*. It is with great joy that I commend this book to you.

As the watchmen of the Lord, we are standing in the breaches and keeping the night vigil for deliverance and revival for our people, our nations, and our world. We hope that you will join us on the wall of prayer in keeping the **Watch of the Lord**™.

Mahesh Chavda
Mahesh Chavda Ministries International
All Nations Church, Charlotte, North Carolina

Introduction

Are you hungry for authentic revival in the land? Does your heart burn with a passion to see Jesus receive the rewards of His suffering? Do you want to do the works of Christ? If so, then I think God had you in mind when He prompted me to write *The Lost Art of Intercession.*

I need to tell you from the start that I am determined to infect you with a holy disease and a righteous obsession. I hope you become a total *prayeraholic!* I believe God wants to see a whole generation of humble, priestly people rise up with the passion and anointing to lay hold of God as He has laid hold of them. I desperately want to see this dream come to pass.

You should also know that nowhere in the Scriptures will you find "the *gift* of intercession" listed, described, or even mentioned! You will find nine gifts of the Spirit described in First Corinthians 12, along with the leadership or equipping gifts described in Ephesians chapter 4, and a mix of the two in the Book of Romans. Yet nowhere is intercession termed a "gift" or "grace." Why? Because it is the *privilege* and *household duty* of every priest in God's Kingdom of priests and kings. It is what you were reborn to do!

As you read these words, Jesus Christ continuously intercedes for you and the Church before His Father. *And He invites you to do the same.* According to Romans 8:34 and Hebrews 7:25, this ministry of intercession is continuous and unbroken.

Jesus, our magnificent obsession, is our most excellent advocate (defense attorney, representative, and go-between) with the Father. He took His stand between us and our sin, and He remains the Intercessor who stands between us and our arch enemy, satan. He personally identified with our total depravity and took upon Himself the sins of every human generation. Then Jesus, the unblemished and guiltless Lamb of God, carried our sin to the cross and forever removed it by dying the death of the guilty man of sin so we would be free. He has done it all!

What if this glorious Christ decided to *act like us* for one moment? What if He folded His arms today and told the Father, "I already did My part. I'm not going to do anything any more"? No, the Scriptures say God's tireless Son "...is able to save forever those who draw near to God through Him, since He always lives to make intercession for them" (Heb. 7:25).

Jesus Christ wants you and I to join Him there in the Father's Presence. Will you join Him in "this road less traveled"? He is searching throughout the earth for spiritual adventurers who will search and excavate for lost treasures of the Holy kind. Will you pay the price to help restore the glory of God to the earth? Do you want to join me? Then read on, brave soul. This book was written just for you.

Chapter 1

Restoring the Moravian Fire

Like Ezekiel of old who sat in the valley filled with old bones, we were sitting in a great cemetery filled with gravestones that marked the resting place of hundreds of Moravian saints. These nearly forgotten prayer warriors had pioneered some of the richest and most daring missionary work in the history of the Church, but on this day all was silent.

Drawn there by a prophetic mission on that pleasant afternoon in February of 1993, 19 intercessors, including my wife Michal Ann and myself, paused for prayer before completing our walk through the cemetery. Our goal was to reach the ancient wooden prayer tower overlooking the cemetery and the Moravian village of Herrnhut, which are located on the northern border of the Czech Republic. While sitting in the cemetery during that time of somber prayer, the Lord spoke to my heart, "Son of man, can these bones live?"

And I responded with the same answer given by Ezekiel thousands of years before me, "Sovereign Lord, You alone know."

Moments later, we quietly left the cemetery and climbed the hill to the prayer tower. After I unlocked the door, we climbed a spiral staircase to the circular mezzanine at the top of the Moravian watch tower. From that vantage point, we could see far beyond the borders of eastern Germany into the neighboring Czech Republic and Poland, but some invisible hand seemed to draw us all away from simply viewing. As we silently gathered together in a loose circle, we could sense a weightiness and deep anticipation growing in our hearts. Something was about to happen...

Suddenly, every person in the tower was overwhelmed with a compelling spirit of intercession unlike anything we had ever experienced. As we prayed, agonized, and groaned under the obvious influence of the Holy Spirit, a strong wind suddenly blew about the tower where we were standing, whipping away hats and scarves in its power. We all knew that this natural phenomenon was an outward manifestation of a mighty movement by the Spirit of God.

> **We had called forth the winds of God's anointing, and that wind was blowing among us. We sensed it bore with it the same anointing that God once gave to the Moravian prayer warriors of the 18th century!**

As one person, we were gripped in deep, groaning travail. We knew what was happening. We had traveled tens of thousands of miles as a team and experienced incredible provision and guidance all along our journey to fulfill the Holy Spirit's command. Our mission was to seek God for the anointing of the spirit of prayer that once rested upon Count Nikolaus Ludwig von Zinzendorf and the Moravian community of faith. Now, just as the prophet Ezekiel called forth the winds of God in Ezekiel 37, we had called forth the winds of God's anointing, and that wind was blowing among us. We sensed it bore with it the same anointing that God once gave to the Moravian prayer warriors of the eighteenth century!

When the wind died down, we waited. Was our mission complete? Was it over as quickly as it began? Somehow we all knew that God wasn't finished with us yet. We confirmed it later, but at the time we sensed that as a woman in the midst of giving birth, we were in a lull between "contractions." Suddenly, we were hit spontaneously as one person with an even stronger spirit of travail, and a second wind began to roar across the valley and up the prayer tower mezzanine where we were positioned. I sensed that this second wind had brought a new wave of faith and anointing to fulfill a holy mandate to blow this spirit of prayer out into the nations.

Immediately, I felt an impression "light up" inside of me that God wanted to raise up the "house of prayer for all nations" in 120 cities, just as He breathed His Spirit into the 120 prayer warriors on the day of Pentecost (see Mt. 21:13; Acts 2). From those 120 cities of prayer, God intended to cover the earth with His glory. Nearly everything in my life had been leading up to that divine appointment with God in Herrnhut. At that moment I knew the rest of my days would be influenced by what transpired that day in a tower above the graves of Count von Zinzendorf and the Moravian brethren.

Three Stands of Truth

What did the believers at Herrnhut have that we don't have today? Long before I ever set foot in the Czech Republic (formerly part of Czechoslovakia) for the first time, I had read books and articles describing the Christian community commonly called the Moravians. Their story is intertwined with the lives and ministries of some of the most important church leaders in the Great Awakenings and revivals that transformed Western society in the eighteenth century. I learned that God gave them "three strands" around which they wove their lives, and these strands helped the Moravians become world-changers:

1. They had relational unity, spiritual community, and sacrificial living.
2. The power of their persistent prayer produced a divine passion and zeal for missionary outreach to the lost. Many of them even sold themselves into slavery in places like Surinam in South America just so they could carry the light of the gospel into closed societies. The Moravians were the first missionaries to the slaves of St. Thomas

in the Virgin Islands; they went to strange places called Lapland and Greenland and to many places in Africa.
3. The third strand was described by a motto that they lived by: "No one works unless someone prays." This took the form of a corporate commitment to sustained prayer and ministry to the Lord. This prayer went on unbroken for 24 hours a day, seven days a week, every day of each year for over 100 years!

The Moravians' over 100-year prayer vigil and global missionary exploits marked one of the purest moves of the Spirit in church history, and it radically changed the expression of Christianity in their age. Many leaders today feel that virtually every great missionary endeavor of the eighteenth and nineteenth centuries—regardless of denominational affiliation—was in a very real sense part of the fruit of the Moravians' sacrificial service and prophetic intercessory prayer. Their influence continues to be felt even in our day. The Lord is clearly planning to increase that influence once again.

Just as the 120 believers tarrying in the upper room in Jerusalem on Pentecost were "baptized in fire" by the Holy Spirit of promise, so those who answer God's call to tarry before His face will also be baptized with a holy fire. The group of believers who gathered at Herrnhut to pursue their dream of religious freedom were in much the same state as most Christians are today. They came from widely diverse religious backgrounds. During the first five years of their communal existence after the community's founding in 1722, they experienced bickering, dissension, and strife. They were no better or worse than you or I, but they made a deep commitment to Jesus Christ and to prayer, which transformed and changed them forever. They began to think God-sized thoughts and feel a burning God-like compassion for the lost. They received supernatural faith to tackle challenges that would in many cases cost them their freedom or their very lives. Yet, they did it all in faithfulness and joy. The Moravians changed the world because they allowed God to change them. God wants to change the world again and He is looking at you and me. Are you willing to seek the same fire that inspired the Moravian believers two centuries ago?

The joy and peaceful confidence that the Moravians exhibited in the face of adversity and death was legendary. "Count von Zinzendorf taught the Moravians to be God's troubadours: They first looked at the Cross and rejoiced because they found there a covering for all their sins. Zinzendorf once declared: 'We are the Saviour's happy people' ... The Moravians have been called the 'Easter People,' and perhaps no other body of Christians has so compellingly expressed their adoration of the risen Lamb."[1]

Wesley's Encounter

John Wesley first encountered Moravians during a stormy ocean voyage. Their influence was destined to forever transform his life and ultimately helped launch the Great Awakening that swept through England and America! Author and prophetic teacher, Rick Joyner, recently published a booklet entitled, *Three Witnesses*, which describes the miraculous work of the Moravians along with their effect on John Wesley in particular:

"During January 1736, Wesley was on a ship bound for America that also carried a number of Moravian missionaries. He was challenged by their great seriousness and their humility in performing for other passengers the most servile tasks, which none of the English passengers would do. When they were offered pay for this, they refused, replying that "it was good for their proud hearts," and "their loving Savior had done more for them." Some of the passengers abused them terribly, even striking them or knocking them down, but they would never strike back or even take offense."

Many perceived these German missionaries to be cowards until a great storm broke over the ship. As the main sail split and the sea began to pour into the ship, the English panicked, their terrified screams rising even above the tumult of the storm. Yet the

Moravians sat quietly, singing their hymns. Afterward, when one of the Moravians was asked if he was afraid during the storm, he answered, "I thank God, no." Then he was asked if their women and children were afraid, and he replied, "No; our women and children are not afraid to die." Wesley recorded this in his diary and added:

> "From them (the Moravians) I went to their crying, trembling neighbors, and pointed out to them the difference in the hour of trial, between him that feareth God, and him that feareth not. At twelve the wind fell. This was the most glorious day which I have hitherto seen."[2]

Wesley knew that he didn't possess what he saw in those simple people of faith, those people called Moravians. He was an ordained minister, yet he hadn't even received Christ as his Savior. He was fascinated by the Moravians' confidence in the face of impending death. He knew that he didn't have what they had, and he decided he wanted it—whatever it was.

The fire of the Moravian believers seemed to ignite hunger for God wherever they went. That hunger could only be satisfied by an encounter with the living God they served. Would to God that every believer, missionary, and minister today would walk, work, and worship with the same fire that the Moravians carried with them to countless cultures and cities!

John Wesley was an ordained minister, yet he hadn't even received Christ as his Savior. He was fascinated by the Moravians' confidence in the face of impending death. He knew that he didn't have what they had, and he decided he wanted it—whatever it was.

God is out to ignite that fire again! Only this time He wants to see His fire roar across entire continents and cultures through the means of His whole body, the Church. As you read these words, the Spirit of God is igniting hearts around the world, drawing believers to their knees and sinners to the cross. He is out to cover the earth with the Father's glory, but He has been commissioned to do it through the transformed lives of fallen human beings who have been redeemed by the blood of Jesus Christ, the Lamb of God.

There is an incident involving Aaron, the priest and the fire of God that pictures the burden of my heart for this book and the work of God in this generation. It is found in Numbers 16:

And the Lord spoke to Moses, saying, "Get away from among this congregation, that I may consume them instantly." Then they fell on their faces. And Moses said to Aaron, "Take your censer and put in it fire from the altar, and lay incense on it; then bring it quickly to the congregation and make atonement for them, for wrath has gone forth from the Lord, the plague has begun!" Then Aaron took it as Moses had spoken, and ran into the midst of the assembly, for behold, the plague had begun among the people. So he put on the incense and made atonement for the people. And he took his stand between the dead and the living, so that the plague was checked. But those who died by the plague were 14,700, besides those who died on account of Korah (Numbers 16:44-49).

Aaron provides a vivid picture of the intercessor. When the congregation of Israel sinned by rebelling against their leaders, God sent a judgment upon them in the form of a plague that killed nearly 15,000 people. Far more would have died, but Moses told Aaron, the high priest, to quickly put fire from God's altar into his censer, or container, along with incense. Then Aaron literally ran out into the midst of the congregation with the fire of God. The Scripture says that Aaron "took his stand between the dead and the living." The fragrant smoke ascending from the burning censer, as Aaron swung it to and fro, formed a line of demarcation between two groups—the dead and the living.

What Are the Applications for Today?

What does that mean for us? I attended a Russian Orthodox service in an effort to better understand the principles in this Old

Testament passage. The word, *cantor,* refers to a priest who prays and sings chants. If you have ever heard a Gregorian chant sung with power and anointing, then you know how beautiful and absolutely incredible the song of a cantor can be. The cantor has a censer or a cantor, a container, a can that is filled with incense. Throughout the cantor's ministry, it continually releases a sweet fragrance and smoke that will fill the sanctuary. Many times this cantor-priest will be dressed in royal priestly regalia as he walks among the people with his instruments of sacrifice (the censer and incense). I remember the Russian Orthodox cantor singing from the Psalms in high praise, "The Lord is good. And His mercy endures forever."

> **God wants His Kingdom of kings and priests to once again take the fire from His Presence and rush it with godly zeal to the people in need. All you have to do is find an "altar" where the fire of God is burning along with an abundant supply of sweet incense.**

Then I heard the people say with one voice, "Amen. The Lord is good, and His mercy endures forever. Amen."

What I saw in the Orthodox service was what I believe to be a very accurate picture of what Aaron did. However, on the day of the crisis when Aaron stepped close to the shekinah Presence of God in the Holy of Holies to take of the fire on the altar, I believe he became consumed with the zeal of the Lord of Hosts and he became a radical!

That is what God wants to do with you and me, and with everyone who calls upon the name of the Lord. He wants to break off the power of intimidation in our lives and cast down the spirit of fear that rejects and avoids the unknown. I once heard my friend, Paul Cain, one of the leading prophetic statesmen of our day, say, "One of the problems we have is that we are so afraid of wildfire that we have no fire." God wants His Kingdom of kings and priests to once again take the fire from His Presence and rush it with godly zeal to the people in need. All you have to do is find an "altar" where the fire of God is burning along with an abundant supply of sweet incense. He wants to transform our generation through His shekinah glory, just as He transformed Aaron.

God wants to use more than a Moses or an Aaron today. One of the unique things about the Church of the New Covenant is that God has authorized and commanded *every believer* to do the work of the ministry! "Point people," or church leaders, can't do it all—in fact, their primary job or reason for being according to the apostle Paul, is "for the equipping of the saints for the work of service, to the building up of the body of Christ" (Eph. 4:12). God wants an entire army of workers out doing the vital work of the ministry and building up His body, the Church.

The plague in Numbers chapter 16 was stopped because Aaron stood in the gap. That is the classic definition of an intercessor: "one who stands in the gap for another." Aaron stood in the gap for his generation, and the plague was stopped. There is a devilish plague running rampant today through our churches, cities, and nations. Now the Lord is calling for a priestly people to rise up and personally carry the holy fire of His Presence to their generation for their salvation and His glory.

Who Will Stand in the Gap?

Let me bring this a little closer to home: God wants to put His Spirit upon you in such a measure that you will answer His summons with a resounding: "Yes, I will stand in the gap for my generation right here and now. I will put aside every pathetic intimidation and every entanglement of namby-pamby religion. I am going to make a difference by willingly taking up the cross of an intercessor. I will lay aside my life for the sake of others before God."

God is restoring the ancient fire that once inspired the Moravians to launch what in their day was the greatest missionary campaign since the Book of Acts. He is restoring His fire to you and me in this generation because He wants us to reap His harvest. The first step begins with the restoration of the fire on God's altar.

Endnotes

1. Anthony J. Lewis, *Zinzendorf the Ecumenical Pioneer* (London: S.C.M. Press, 1962), 73-74.

2. Rick Joyner, *Three Witnesses* (Charlotte, North Carolina: Morningstar Publications, 1997), 56.

Chapter 2

Restoring the Fire on the Altar

Fire shall be kept burning continually on the altar; it is not to go out (Leviticus 6:13).

Several years ago the Lord called me aside to spend nearly a month with Him in "solitary confinement." His purpose was clear: He wanted to place me in an intensive "Mary position" so I could hear clearly what He wanted to say to me.[1] I didn't realize it then, but the words I would hear at the end of those weeks of isolated prayer would lay part of the foundation for my ministry during the remainder of this decade, and for this book as well. I came to learn later that He was also saying the same thing to other members of His Body around the world.

I suspended my travel itinerary and positioned myself far from the nearest telephone. (The voice I needed to hear did not need a telephone or FAX machine to reach me.) During that period, I spent precious hours waiting on the Lord, and He blessed me again and again as I sat at His feet and listened for His every word. At the end of my prayer consecration, the Holy Spirit gave me an order from the Father's throne: "It's time for *fire on the altar*." I had been awakened in the night a few months earlier, and for two hours my mind had been filled with eight phrases that kept circulating in my thoughts as I sought God's face: "Blazing altars ... the fire and the altar ... altars ablaze ... flaming altars ... the altar and the flame ... altars aflame ... altars on fire." The one phrase that struck me the most was, "Fire on the altar." I didn't realize it at the time, but this was an exact quote of a portion of Leviticus 6:9, which says, "Command Aaron and his sons, saying, 'This is the law for the burnt offering: the burnt offering itself shall remain on the hearth on the altar all night until the morning, and the *fire on the altar* is to be kept burning on it.'"

> **Count von Zinzendorf knew the fire of the altar signified the *prayer of the saints*, and he viewed this word as a literal command to restore unceasing prayer before the Lord. Church history, and, therefore, world history, would never be the same again.**

This is followed four verses later by the summary command, "Fire shall be kept burning continually on the altar; it is not to go out" (Lev. 6:13). According to Professor Leslie K. Tarr, this is the verse Count von Zinzendorf received from the Holy Spirit in 1727 which inspired the Moravian's incredible 100-year prayer vigil launched that year.[2] The Count realized that this reference referred to the altar of sacrifice, but he also understood that this Old Testament priestly function involving fire and sacrifices carried a much greater and abiding significance on this side of the cross. He knew the fire of the altar signified the *prayer of the saints*, and he viewed this word as a literal command to restore unceasing prayer before the Lord. Church history, and, therefore, world history, would never be the same again.

One of the weaknesses I perceive in many North American churches today is a profound ignorance and even a disdain at times of the Old Testament Scriptures. It is not surprising that few American believers understand the Book of Hebrews or the many references of Jesus Christ that come from the Old Testament. Any one who longs to walk closer to God must embrace *all* of His

Word, including the books of the Old Testament. Count von Zin-zendorf's revelation from the Book of Leviticus is an important example of how God can use shadows and types from Old Testament relationships and dealings to reveal and enlighten us on His work today.

According to the instructions Aaron, the high priest, received through Moses in Leviticus chapter 16, before the high priest could pass through the inner veil into the Most Holy Place or Holy of Holies, he was to minister at two stations in the outer court and three within the Holy Place. First, he would offer up the sacrifice of blood at the brazen altar. This was followed by the ceremonial washing of water at the laver. After entering the Holy Place through the outer veil, the priest would approach the lamp stand (holding seven golden candlesticks). The table of shew-bread preceded a golden altar of incense which rested immediately in front of the inner veil. Beyond the veil in the Most Holy Place was the ark of the covenant, with the mercy seat flanked by its covering cherubs. This was the place of communion—the place where God's Presence was manifested and His glory was made known.

God's Prophetic Calendar

Where do we stand corporately in God's prophetic time table? The stations of service in the tabernacle of Moses perfectly picture the progressive work of God to perfect His Bride in the earth. The Protestant reformation restored the spiritual truths depicted by the brazen altar and its blood sacrifice. This simple yet profound understanding of justification by faith in the blood of Christ is the beginning place in our journey into the presence of God.

In the 1800s, John Wesley and the Holiness Movement helped to reclaim the spiritual truths of the laver: the place of cleansing and sanctification. At the turn of the century, the Pentecostal Revival returned the emphasis of the power and the gifts of the Spirit as represented in the lamp stand (or the seven golden candlesticks). Sixty years later this was followed by the Charismatic

Renewal, which highlighted the fellowship of breaking bread as exhibited in the table of shewbread.

Perhaps today, in God's progressive plan of unfolding truth, we find ourselves ministering at the altar of incense. As the New Testament priesthood of believers, we are prophetically swinging the censor of praise and prayers unto the Lord Most High. Today, we stand collectively before the altar of incense and the time for lighting our incense has come!

A Life-Changing Event

In January 1993, I traveled to the Czech Republic with a group of intercessors to join the believers there in "christening" their new nation to the Lord.. While standing on the platform before Dan Drapal's Christian Fellowship of Prague, a series of words seemed to fall into my mind. "Have you considered the multi-directional dimension of prayer?" This sentence captured my attention but I did not have time to ponder it, as it was time for me to deliver my next statement. Then the words, "Remember, what goes up must come down!" burst into my conscience. What was the Lord trying to tell me? Does prayer have more than one direction? My thoughts quickly were then taken to Revelation 8:3-5:

> *And another angel came and stood at the altar, holding a golden censer; and much incense was given to him, that he might add it to the prayers of all the saints upon the golden altar which was before the throne. And the smoke of the incense, with the prayers of the saints, went up before God out of the angel's hand. And the angel took the censer; and he filled it with the fire of the altar and threw it to the earth; and there followed peals of thunder and sounds and flashes of lightning and an earthquake* (Revelation 8:3-5).

I could begin to see it. *What goes up does come down!* Our prayers arise from our humble earthly habitation unto their heavenly destination. The angels, acting as altar attendants, take their censers and fill them with much incense (which is the prayers of the saints). The angels become the heavenly cantors, swinging our prayers and praises before our Lord. Then they take the censers and fill them with the *fire on the altar* and throw it back down on the earth. Signs and wonders follow as what went up is cast back down on the earth.

One of these "wonders" that is specifically listed in Revelation 8 is lightning. Amazing, isn't it? Nearly a year later, God gave me another piece to the puzzle in a powerful dream I received in Toronto, Ontario. It concerned the "downward fire" of the godly equation, "What goes up must come down." I was conducting my second "Fire on the Altar Conference" at a Vineyard Fellowship in Cambridge, a suburb of Toronto in December of 1993. My last night, in the basement guest room of the pastor's house, I had a dream in which I saw hundreds of consecutive lightning bolts splintering and showering down on the earth from the heavens. There weren't any people or spoken words in the dream, just this brilliant shower of lightening bolts continuously striking the earth.

I don't know what time it was, but some time that night I awoke from the dream and realized that the room was filled with what I call "the destiny of God." Then, with my eyes wide open, I saw large letters measuring two or three feet high hanging in the room, and they said, "Job 36:32." I just waited quietly in the room and after awhile I turned on the light and reached for my Bible. I was thrilled and puzzled by what I read in verse 32 and the following verse.

He covers His hands with the lightning, and commands it to strike the mark. Its noise declares His presence; the cattle also, concerning what is coming up. At this also my heart trembles, and leaps from its place. Listen closely to the thunder of His voice, and the rumbling that goes out from His mouth. Under the whole heaven He lets it loose, and His lightning to the ends of the earth (Job 36:32-37:3).

God covers His hands with *lightning* and He sends it forth and it strikes the mark. Although these are the words of Elihu, they sure seem to agree with the picture of God's fire in Revelation 8:3-5. Later I came to learn that the Hebrew word translated as "strikes the mark" is *paga*. This same word is translated as "intercession" in Isaiah 59:16, where God laments in the Messianic passage, "And He saw that there was no man, and was astonished that there was no one to *intercede* [*paga*]; then His own arm brought salvation to Him; and His righteousness upheld Him."

Intercession releases God's brilliant light or lightning to "strike the mark" in the earth, directing God's power and glory into desired situations with supernatural results! A friend sent me a lengthy study of lightning in the Bible and suggested that lightning is the anointed Word of God going forth from the mouth of the saints. He believed the Scriptures imply that as we speak the Word of God, it goes forth from our mouth like lightning to intercede and strike the mark, routing our enemies and bringing the judgment of God to situations, laying bare the hearts of men, and fully accomplishing whatever God commanded it to accomplish. I have to agree that this is totally in line with the Bible as I understand it.

The Power of God's Word

When God's Word goes forth, channels of living water appear in the midst of barren deserts. God's Word lights up everything, and nothing can hide from its illuminating power. Demonic powers tremble and melt at its presence. When God's Word is sent forth in faith and obedience, it will cause people around us to see God's glory.

Another picture of this dynamic function of *paga* is that intercession "paints the targets" so God can zero in on areas of need with His glory! He sets His "gun sights" on these targets and "strikes the mark" with His lightning or "displays of His brilliant presence."[3] We have the privilege of painting targets on cities, nations, churches, and individuals granting access points to the one whose hands are covered with light. By this, we call light to overcome darkness. This dream of the continuous shower of lightning bolts from Heaven came in December of 1993, seven weeks before the outbreak of the Spirit began after the Lord sent Randy Clark to what was then the Toronto Airport Vineyard Christian Fellowship. Since then, the rain of God's Presence on that region has been continuous. A pastor's wife from the state of Washington was in a service in Toronto and "under the influence" of the Holy Spirit when the voice of the Lord whispered to her and said: "Do you remember all of the prayers that you have prayed for revival? This is the beginning of that." Since then, even the secular media has discovered the fires of God roaring out from places like Toronto, Pensacola, and London.

> **Intercession "paints the targets" so God can zero in on areas of need with His glory! He sets His "gun sights" on these targets and "strikes the mark" with His lightning or "displays of His brilliant presence."**

Not only is it amazing and astounding that our prayers affect the destiny of individuals and nations, but God would also say to us: "Rejoice that you are given the magnificent privilege of ministering to Me at this most precious heavenly altar! Rejoice that the altar of incense is that which is nearest to My heart." Oh what a blessed gift and privilege is this holy thing called prayer!

More than anything else, prayer is man's invitation sent heavenward for God's response to be cast earthward—the human in exchange for the heavenly!

Second Chronicles 7:1-3 gloriously depicts this principle:

Now when Solomon had finished praying, fire came down from heaven and consumed the burnt offering and the sacrifices; and the glory of the Lord filled the house. And the priests could not enter into the house of the Lord, because the glory of the Lord filled the Lord's house. And all the sons of Israel, seeing the fire come down and the glory of the Lord upon the house, bowed down on the pavement

*with their faces to the ground, and they worshiped and
gave praise to the Lord, saying, "Truly He is good, truly
His lovingkindness is everlasting"* (2 Chronicles 7:1-3).

This is what we yearn for! We have seen it happen here and
there—in Toronto, London, and Pensacola, and then in many other
cities across the globe. But we must have more, Lord! We want to
see God's glory fill the earth. *It will happen through exchange.*
Prayer ascends. Incense arises. Man's smoke signal to His Highest Chief arises declaring, "Send forth the fire!" Heavenly fire
from the altar then comes crashing down and the glory of the
Lord fills His house once again. What goes up must come down.

Let's present ourselves on God's altar as our spiritual service
of worship. (See Romans 12.) Let's offer up the continual sacrifices of praise and the incense of prayer. And let us continue to do
so until the angels take their censer, fill it to the brim, and cast
Heaven's *fire on the altar* back down into our earthly dwelling
places again.

Even so, let the fire on the altar come tumbling forth. Let
God's priests prostrate themselves before Him. May His glory in-
vade and pervade His house until all God's people cry, "Amen
and Amen!"

Following the Blueprint

The Old Testament "blueprint" of the tabernacle of Moses reveals an ancient and divine pattern marking the methodical restoration of truth and practice in Church history. The tabernacle was
divided into three areas, and each area was equipped with specific
pieces of furniture for specific purposes. The path to God's Presence required the high priest of the Old Testament to move pro-
gressively from the outer court into the inner court (the Holy
Place), and ultimately through the veil into the Holy of Holies, or
the Most Holy Place. These steps of progressive revelation have
a striking parallel to God's plan of restoration for His Son's
Bride, the Church:

The Outer Court—Where Sinful Man
Comes to God in Need of Salvation

A. The Protestant Reformation (Repentance and Forgiveness: First Station of the Lamb)
   1. Restoration of the altar of sacrifice.
   2. Restoration of the sacrifice of the blood.
   3. Restoration of justification by faith.
B. The Holiness Movement (Cleansing and Sanctification: Second Station of the Lamb)
   1. Restoration of the brazen laver.
   2. Restoration of the washing of the hands.
   3. Restoration of cleansing and sanctification.

The Inner Court—The Holy Place (For Priests Only)

C. The Pentecostal Outpouring (Illumination and Anointing: Third Station of the Lamb)
   1. Restoration of the golden lamp stand
   2. Restoration of the lighting and burning of the seven golden candlesticks
   3. Restoration of the power and gifts of the Spirit.
D. The Charismatic Outpouring (The Full Portion of God's Bread: Fourth Station of the Lamb)
   1. Restoration of the table of shewbread.
   2. Restoration of the twelve loaves of bread, representing the twelve tribes of Israel.
   3. Restoration of fellowship across the Body of Christ.
E. The Prayer Movement (Worship and Prayer: Fifth Station of the Lamb)
   1. Restoration of the altar of incense.
   2. Restoration of the fire continually burning on the altar.
   3. Restoration of worship and prayer.

The time of the incense has come! That the altar of incense has its place nearest to the curtain before the Holy of Holies signifies the spiritual specificity of prayer as coming nearest to the heart of God.

Perhaps the "sixth station" of the Lamb will be the unveiling of an entire Church of kings and priests ministering boldly to God Himself within the Most Holy Place—in full view of the unsaved world and the principalities and powers of the air. This would be a literal fulfillment of David's ancient psalm in which he said, "The Lord is my Shepherd, I shall not want ... He setteth a table before me in the presence of mine enemies."

Perhaps the "sixth station" of the Lamb will be the unveiling of an entire church of kings and priests ministering boldly to God Himself within the Most Holy Place—in full view of the unsaved world and the principalities and powers of the air.

I find it interesting that whether you ask people in worship services at Pasadena's Harvest Rock Church, or at Brownsville Assembly of God, or at London's Holy Trinity Brompton Anglican Church, or at any of the places where God's Spirit is being poured out, they will all speak in the same terms. They say they sensed God's glory and Presence overwhelm them. This is one of the ways we experience the "manifest presence of God," which is exactly how the Old Testament describes the Presence that descended on the mercy seat between the golden cherubim of the ark of the covenant in Aaron's day! My friends, the God of Abraham, Isaac, and Jacob is alive and well today. He has arisen to visit His people by sitting in the throne of worship and prayer we have made for Him through our prayer, praise, worship, and intercession!

Sometimes God breaks out of our "theoretical models of prayer." You see, He is not a static God. He is not a "tame" God who is content to stay inside of our neat little theological boxes and paradigms. According to the Scriptures, when we dare to draw nigh unto Him, He will draw nigh unto us (see Jas. 4:8)! That means when you move yourself close to the consuming fire of God, then He will move the fire of His Presence closer to you. That means that you and I are going to feel the heat of God and get fired up too!

Is Your Heart on Fire?

Consider the qualities of fire. In the natural realm, fire purifies, fuels, illuminates, and warms. In the spirit realm, fire is seen as the power of God to judge, sanctify, empower, inspire, enlighten, reveal, and warm the heart. It is time to draw near to the altar of God and stoke the fires of God in our hearts. There is another type of divine response to our uplifted fire and incense in addition to His dispatch of holy lightning to the earth:

...fire came down from heaven and consumed the burnt offering and the sacrifices; and the glory of the Lord filled the house. And the priests could not enter into the house of the Lord, because the glory of the Lord filled the Lord's house (2 Chronicles 7:1-2).

The restoration of the fire on the altar is not an end in itself. It is but the first step in a progression toward our loving God. In the next step, God wants to turn our eyes and hearts outward, from ourselves to others, with compassion like that of our great High Priest and Chief Intercessor.

Endnotes

1. The "Mary Position" is the posture of singleminded worship and yearning, while you are seated at the feet of Jesus with Him as your sole and total point of focus. This is in contrast to the approach of a "Martha." Martha busied herself with the details of work, and she is characterized by much distraction, worry, and care. Her busyness kept her apart from the words and face of Jesus (see Lk. 10:38-42).

2. Leslie K. Tarr, "A Prayer Meeting That Lasted 100 Years," *Decision* Magazine (Billy Graham Evangelistic Association, May 1977). Used by permission.

3. This term, "brilliant Presence," is part of another related vision concerning Gods "highest weapon of spiritual warfare," which I cover in detail in Chapter 6 of this book, entitled "Restoring the Path From Prayer to His Presence."

Chapter 3

Restoring the Priestly Role of Intercession

You also, as living stones, are being built up as a spiritual house for a holy priesthood, to offer up spiritual sacrifices acceptable to God through Jesus Christ (1 Peter 2:5).

Several years ago I was ministering in Phoenix, Arizona, when I saw a vision take form in front of me. I saw a caterpillar that appeared to be weaving something, and I realized it was forming a cocoon around itself. When the time came for this caterpillar to finally emerge from its chrysalis, it had to struggle just to escape its womb of transformation. Nevertheless, as I watched, the creature struggled until it finally emerged as a fully formed butterfly arrayed in brilliant and iridescent colors. When I asked the Lord about what this was, He said, "It is the Church in metamorphosis."

Nearly everyone would agree at this point in time that the Church is in a place of change. But if we are ever to reach the fullness of all that God has prophesied we will be, then we must allow the Holy Spirit to tutor us and lead us to the secret dwelling of the Most High God. It is there in His presence, hidden away from the world's influence, that we are changed into another dimension

and expression of His glory. We *all* have a divine appointment to
be "shut in with God in a secret place." We are a priestly race in
transition. We are called to press into God through Christ and
overcome our fleshly encumbrances and worldly distractions so
we can co-labor with Him to accomplish His plans and purposes.
The Christian life is a life of change, of metamorphosis from the
old to the new, of transformation "from glory to glory" as we
look upon the face of Jesus in the Most Holy Place. Then we will
emerge from our holy seclusion arrayed with His iridescent glory,
fully remade as many-faceted expressions of His love, His nature,
and His glory. We know where and what we are now. But God has
a plan—a bluebrint He is working from. Here is what God's Word
says we should become:

> *And Thou hast made them to be a kingdom and priests to
> our God; and they will reign upon the earth* (Revelation
> 5:10).

> *For if by the transgression of the one, death reigned
> through the one, much more those who receive the abun-
> dance of grace and of the gift of righteousness will reign
> in life through the One, Jesus Christ* (Romans 5:17).

> *I urge you therefore, brethren, by the mercies of God, to
> present your bodies a living and holy sacrifice, acceptable
> to God, which is your spiritual service of worship. And do
> not be conformed to this world, but be transformed by the
> renewing of your mind, that you may prove what the will of
> God is, that which is good and acceptable and perfect*
> (Romans 12:1-2).

If there is one thing that I could plant in your heart, it would
be this: Prayer is not an activity, and it is not an application. It is
life found in a person. Once you see Jesus, once the blinders fall
away from your eyes in the glory of His Presence, your attitudes
about prayer will totally change! This thing of prayer, this thing
of intercession, of standing in the gap, of making an appeal to a

superior—it is not a hard task! It is a joy. It's called life in the Kingdom.

The parallels between the duties of the Old Testament priests who served in the tabernacle of Moses and the priestly mission of believers today are too important to ignore or dismiss. Although the type of sacrifices we offer today and our reasons for offering them are dramatically different, it is still profitable to study the Old Testament priesthood. We can add to our knowledge and understanding of prayer by examining the priestly functions of the sons of Aaron, for those functions were instituted by God, Himself, as a type and shadow of the greater priesthood of Jesus Christ and those who follow Him. Throughout any study of Old Testament patterns, we should remember that every believer is called to be a priest unto the Lord today. Those duties are no longer confined to just a select few, and we need to understand that *there is no greater duty a believer can perform than prayer!* This is a chief function of the believer-priest today.

Removing the Blockades

In September of 1991, I was ministering in New York City with my wife Michal Ann when the Presence of the Holy Spirit came to rest on me early one morning. I began to hear His voice clearly speak the following phrase to me: "I will release new understandings of identification in intercession whereby the legal basis of the rights of the demonic powers of the air to remain will be removed. Then, in that hour My people will speak My Word and I will fell the enemy."

What is this thing, "identification in intercession" anyway? I believe that it is a lost art, and it is perhaps one of the highest, yet most overlooked, aspects of true intercession. It is the ability and function of personally identifying with the needs of others to such an extent that in heart you become one with them by the Holy Spirit. It is expressed as we identify with Jesus and follow in His footsteps, because His footsteps will lead us beyond the four walls of our churches into the streets of a fractured world of prostitutes, crooks, losers, and broken and wounded people—in other words, to real people with real problems. He leads us into a genuine priesthood where we, like our Master and High Priest, can be touched by the infirmities, temptations, and struggles of others (Heb. 4:15). The only way we can genuinely and effectively *intercede* is out of a heart of compassion, contrition, and desperation, from a heart that pounds with the sufferings of others as though they are our own.

> **What is this thing, "identification in intercession" anyway? I believe that it is a lost art, and perhaps one of the highest, yet most overlooked, aspects of true intercession. It is the ability and function of personally identifying with the needs of others to such an extent that in heart you become one of them by the Holy Spirit.**

Through the inward work of the Spirit of revelation, we can identify with God's righteous judgments which are due—and yet experience His searing passion to express His grace and mercy. Our eyes will be opened to the horrifying condition of the people and the specific sins which block their way to the cross. Then, *by choosing to be one with them*, by laying aside our position for the sake of others, our hearts will be burdened by the Spirit of God to utter cries of confession and unspeakable intercession on their behalf. As we from our hearts confess sin, disgrace, failure, and humiliation on their behalf to the Lord, we clear away every obstacle of the enemy so those for whom we labor can, themselves, come to the cross in repentance and restoration.

This form of intercession is a lost art in our modern day materialistic and success-oriented society. We need more people with a heart like the apostle Paul, who wrote in the anguish of a true intercessor:

> *I am telling the truth in Christ, I am not lying, my conscience bearing me witness in the Holy Spirit, that I have great sorrow and unceasing grief in my heart. **For I could wish that I myself were accursed, separated from Christ***

for the sake of my brethren, my kinsmen according to the flesh (Romans 9:1-3).

Let's seek Him for these deeper workings in our lives so that *in our day* the Lord, the Judge of all, will find us standing in the gap for the Church, for our nation, and for the needy and the lost. Perhaps identification in intercession is the wedding of the spirit of revelation, described in Ephesians 1:7-8, with the spirit of conviction described by Jesus, who would convict the world of "sin, and righteousness, and judgment" (see Jn. 16:8).

The Holy Spirit illuminated certain Scriptures with new understanding in the light of the word I received in New York City, particularly this passage in the Book of Isaiah:

And it shall be said, "Build up, build up, prepare the way, Remove every obstacle out of the way of My people." For thus says the high and exalted One Who lives forever, whose name is Holy, "I dwell on a high and holy place, and also with the contrite and lowly of spirit in order to revive the spirit of the lowly and to revive the heart of the contrite" (Isaiah 57:14-15).

The Spirit wants to take Scripture passages like this and wed them with revelation and conviction. Then He will bring to us prophetic revelation and understanding and show how to use God's Word as "holy bulldozers" to push out of the way the obstacle of sin and annul the curse over the land.

Paul wrote, "But whom you forgive anything, I forgive also; for indeed what I have forgiven, if I have forgiven anything, I did it for your sakes in the presence of Christ, in order that *no advantage be taken of us by satan; for we are not ignorant of his schemes*" (2 Cor. 2:10-11). God wants us to pray and intercede with great power and effectiveness, not foolishly striking blindly at the air like a poorly trained boxer (see 1 Cor. 9:26). The Holy Spirit wants to teach us how to "remove the legal basis of the demonic powers of the air to remain," so every devilish obstacle will be removed.

The passion of intercession springs from the heart of Jesus Christ Himself, who said, "Behold, I say to you, lift up your eyes, and look on the fields, that they are white for harvest" (Jn. 4:35b). I think Jesus is saying something here that we don't normally comprehend. If we truly lift up our eyes to see with God's eyes, our vision is going to be filled with the horrifying condition of hurting people who are separated from Christ! In one sense, we don't need to ask God for a special "burden" to go into the fields. We need only open our eyes to see men as God sees them. Then our hearts will be moved with a burning compassion that stems directly from the Father heart of God.

Pictures of Priesthood

The roots of our high priestly ministry extend thousands of years behind us, preceding and foreshadowing the intent of God's invasion of human history through His Son, Jesus Christ. The first priest recorded in Scripture may well have been Adam, who ministered on behalf of God and God's creation in the garden of Eden. Then perhaps we see it in the accepted sacrifice of Abel. But the first individual actually called *kohen*, or priest, was Melchizedek king of Salem:

> ...[who] *brought out bread and wine; now he was a priest of God Most High. And he blessed him and said, "Blessed be Abram of God Most High, Possessor of heaven and earth; and blessed be God Most High, Who has delivered your enemies into your hand. And he gave him a tenth of all* (Genesis 14:18-20).

Even the first priest was careful to minister in two dimensions: to God on behalf of men, and to men on behalf of God. God later established the Aaronic priesthood as part of the instructions He gave to Moses on Mt. Sinai, where He also gave him the law inscribed on stone tablets. He told Moses to build a tent according to very specific guidelines as His portable habitation among His people while they journeyed to the promised land. This tent was called the "tent of God's Presence" and the tabernacle of Moses.

It contained three main concentric areas into which only the priests of the tribe of Levi could enter, and then only after they had made themselves ceremonially clean.

The first area, just inside the curtains of the tent, was the courtyard or "outer place." The largest of the three spaces, it contained the brazen alter and brazen laver where the blood of innocent animal sacrifices without flaws was shed, and where their bodies were offered to God by fire. (The shedding of blood and the sacrifice of the innocent for the guilty in those sacrifices foreshadowed the shedding of Christ's innocent blood and His willing sacrifice on the Cross to take away the sin of the world).

It was at the brazen laver that the bloodied priests washed themselves before moving deeper into the tent. Next was the main tent, a covered area which housed the Holy Place and the enclosed the third area called the Most Holy Place (or Holy of Holies, where God's shekinah glory or Presence resided). These spaces represented levels of holiness on earth. The deeper one moved into the tabernacle, the stricter the requirements for holiness were.

Priests ministering under the old covenant followed a progressive series of rituals to prepare themselves to minister before the Presence of the Holy God in the tabernacle. First, sacrifices of blood were offered for the atonement of sin in the outer court. The priest was required to first come to the place of sacrifice before he could enter the tabernacle and minister to the Lord. Only after Aaron the high priest had made a sacrifice of blood for his sin on the altar and washed himself in the laver could he pass through the first veil into the Holy Place.

When Jesus laid down His life for us and shed His blood on the cross, He atoned for, or paid, for our sin forever, and His shed blood became a flowing fount, a holy laver that cleanses us from all sin. He became the living Way and the eternal Door into the Holy Place of God, where only priests could enter in. In that place, as priests of the Lord, we offer sacrifices of praise, worship, and adoration, guided and bathed by the light of His Word, and sustained by the bread of His Word and the fellowship of His broken body, the Church.

Going Beyond the Veil

Then we pass through the veil into the Holy of Holies and stand before the ark of the covenant where the cherubim of gold hover over the mercy seat, the place of God's manifest Presence. The mercy seat is barely visible through the sweetly fragrant smoke of the incense of our prayers, praise, and worship. Only the high priest could enter this place in the days before the cross, and then only once a year on the Day of Atonement.

> **Each function of the Aaronic priesthood represents a truth about man's relationship with God that we need to understand in the light of the cross.**

The functions of the Old Testament priests foreshadow the greater reality God longs to see manifested in His priestly people today. The writer of Hebrews declares, "But now He [Jesus Christ] has obtained a more excellent ministry, by as much as He is also the mediator of a better covenant, which has been enacted on better promises" (Heb. 8:6). Then he carefully compares what I term "the glory of the former house" (the Jews' relationship to God through the law and animal sacrifice) to "the glory of the latter house" (the relationship of all men to God the Father through the blood of His Son, the Lamb of God, Jesus Christ).

Each function of the Aaronic priesthood represents a truth about man's relationship with God that we need to understand in the light of the cross.

1. In the Old Testament, only the high priest could enter the place of God's "residence" and have fellowship with Him. Under the new covenant executed by the death of Jesus Christ, *every believer is a priest.*
2. The priests of old knew God ritually, and in a relationship that was bound in fear without a revelation of love.

Today, every believer can know God intimately and personally in a relationship marked by love, mercy, and grace.

3. The seemingly endless sacrifices of the old covenant had to be repeated each time the priest entered the tabernacle. Today, we have ready access to God anytime and all the time through the blood of Jesus, who paid the debt for our sin once and for all. Our sins are covered by His blood, and He has set us aside for Himself (sanctified us) as His prized possession, His Bride.

4. The descendants of Abraham knew God as the invisible Spirit who lived in a tent (and for a short time, in a stone house). Today, God has fulfilled His promise and He no longer resides in a tent. He lives among men, instead, dwelling in our hearts in the person of the Holy Spirit. This same Spirit reveals God to every believer on a personal level, and we have intimate fellowship with God as a result.

The priestly functions of the Old Testament point us to our duties as the children of God in the New Testament. We now have been made priests and kings in the line of the Messiah as sons and daughters of God. However, our priesthood still includes the instruments of the cross and an altar of sacrifice, just as it was for our Lord!

And He was saying to them all, "If anyone wishes to come after Me, let him deny himself, and take up his cross daily, and follow Me. For whoever wishes to save his life shall lose it, but whoever loses his life for My sake, he is the one who will save it" (Luke 9:23-24).

I urge you therefore, brethren, by the mercies of God, to present your bodies a living and holy sacrifice, acceptable to God, which is your spiritual service of worship. And do not be conformed to this world, but be transformed by the renewing of your mind, that you may prove

*what the will of God is, that which is good and acceptable
and perfect* (Romans 12:1-2).

God intended all along to form for Himself a Kingdom of
priests and kings. He has always longed to fellowship with us at
the altar of incense. Now He longs to call us closer, beyond the
veil of separation, so He can meet and commune with us in the
Most Holy Place of His manifest Presence. So you see, the
Aaronic priesthood of the Old Testament was just a shadow of
what God really longed to do once the Sacrificed Lamb com-
pleted His mission of redemption.

Types and shadows or not, certain aspects of the priesthood of
old were nevertheless ordained to carry over into our day. In
Leviticus 16, God gave Moses very detailed instructions about
the laws of atonement and the priestly progression into God's
presence, and they contain something you and I need to understand in our day:

*And he shall take a firepan full of coals of fire from upon
the altar before the Lord, and two handfuls of finely
ground sweet incense, and bring it inside the veil. And he
shall put the incense on the fire before the Lord, that the
cloud of incense may cover the mercy seat that is on the
ark of the testimony, lest he die* (Leviticus 16:12-13).

*Command the sons of Israel that they bring to you clear
oil from beaten olives for the light, to make a lamp burn
continually. Outside the veil of testimony in the tent of
meeting, Aaron shall keep it in order from evening to
morning before the Lord continually; it shall be a perpetual statute throughout your generations* (Leviticus 24:2-3).

These ordinances for the Holy Place and the Most Holy Place
speak of "perpetual statutes for all generations." Perpetual *still*
means forever, even in our generation. Did God not mean what
He said? But I thought we were under a new covenant. All things
are new; the old has passed away. So what does God mean by
"forever" in this context?

Out of the Shadows Into the Light

God no longer requires us to keep vigil over a fire in a tent or stone temple, but the reality revealed in the principle remains perpetual. The sacrifices we should offer to the Lord as priests and kings include sacrifices of thanksgiving, praise, worship, unceasing prayer, and the service of intercession. That is why it is necessary for God to issue a call to intercession as a vital part of any effort to restore the priesthood of all believers to His Church. There is no way around it: Every priest of God is called and anointed to pray and intercede. A prayerless priest isn't a priest. Just as the prayers and intercession of Aaron with the incense and fire from the altar saved the lives of thousands the day Korah rebelled in Numbers 16, so do our prayers and intercession make the difference for people today!

Did you realize that nowhere in the Scriptures is prayer, praise, worship, and intercession technically called a special spirit gift? It's not there—nowhere to be found! Do you inow why? It's the right of every priest! God is an equal opportunity employer, and the ministry of prayer and praise is the job description of every authentic priest.

> Every priest of God is called and anointed to pray and intercede. A prayerless priest isn't a priest. Just as the prayers and intercession of Aaron with the incense and fire from the altar saved the lives of thousands the day Korah rebelled in Numbers 16, so do our prayers and intercession make the difference for people today!

Defining Our Terms

According to Merriam-Webster, the word *intercede* means "to intervene between parties with a view to reconciling differences: mediate."[1] The Latin root words mean basically "to go between." As we noted in the previous chapter, the Hebrew word for intercession in the Messianic passage of Isaiah 59:16 is *paga*. It

literally means to "strike the mark." The importance of intercession in our day can't be overestimated, yet satan has been very
successful in his attempts to convince Christians that prayer is
mostly a useless exercise in futility. To action-oriented Americans
in particular, prayer seems to be the silliest thing they could do in
times of crisis, stress, or emergency. Jesus thought otherwise.
Throughout the Gospels, we find Jesus disappearing to spend entire nights in fervent prayer before ministering to the masses the
following day. He chose to spend His last night before the cruci-
fixion in the Garden of Gethsemane—praying. In our day, there
are countless stories of supernatural intervention through the
power of prayer and intercession.

The Power of Incense

Jackie Pullinger-Toa is a wonderful, radical missionary states-
woman serving the Lord in Hong Kong. At the age of 19 she was
overcome with a passion to serve God. Though she didn't know
where it was going to be, she just offered herself up uncondition-
ally to Him for His service. God told her to get on a particular
boat so she got on the boat, not knowing where it was taking her.
She got off in Hong Kong and was taken to a place called the
"Walled City." There she met a man who was a kingpin of the
drug lords in the Walled City. He had a brother named Alie who
was studying to be a Buddhist monk. Alie was also facing court
charges as an alleged accomplice with seven other men in the
murder of a rival drug lord.

Jackie began to visit this particular Hong Kong jail every
week to minister and to testify to these men, and specifically to
Alie. Four of the men came to the Lord almost immediately. But
though Jackie visited the jail every day for nine months testify-
ing to Alie about Jesus through a thick glass partition, he was
unmoved.

Alie wouldn't admit it, but he was very afraid of dying for a
crime that he did not do. Week after week, Jackie Pullinger-Toa
continued to minister to him. "I know that you are afraid, Alie. I
know that you are terrified of death, but I want to tell you that

there is a loving God. There is a God of justice who knows all things and He is a Father of mercy. And I have enlisted Christians from all across the world to pray and fast on every Wednesday for you, Alie." Although Alie heard and understood the things Jackie was saying, he still refused to come to the Lord because his heart was hard.

One day the governor of the jail and a jail attendant passed by Alie's cell and remarked to one another that they smelled something. They did not know what the strange fragrance was, but they thought it was some kind of delicate perfume with a fragrant odor. They began asking Alie questions about the fragrance, but Alie said, "What smell?" Perplexed, the two men asked other inmates about the smell, as the entire jail cell took on the fragrant odor of this strange perfume.

Finally, the governor of the jail sent authorities into Alie's cell. They searched his body and found nothing. When they sniffed the air around him, they nodded and said, "Yes, the smell is here." Yet Alie still smelled nothing. When the guards left, Alie began to ask himself, *What is that smell?* Then a little word trickled down inside him. It was this simple message: "Oh, it is Wednesday!" Suddenly, he remembered Jackie's words. *He was smelling prayer!* He realized his entire jail cell was filled with the fragrant aroma of the prayers of the saints.

As Jackie continued to visit Alie, they talked of these things. One day Alie accepted Jesus as Jackie prayed for him through the glass partition. The Holy Spirit came upon him and Alie began to speak in another language. The time came for his court trial. Alie went before the judge, who released him without ever hearing the case!

The Fragrance of Prayer

Alie was saved because of the prayers offered to God on his behalf. So many prayers were directed at him in his tiny jail cell that the air was saturated with the sweet incense of intercession. When believers from all over the world began to exercise their priestly duties and offer the incense of intercession before the

Presence of the Lord, the air in that Hong Kong prison cell was so filled with prayer that even unbelievers could smell their fragrance! The fruit of that prayer was that Alie surrendered his life to Jesus. Is anyone smelling your prayers? Can anyone tell what day it is by the fragrance of your intercession?

The laws of God are immutable, including the natural laws of gravity. "What goes up must come down!" The law of gravity applies here. In the days of Aaron, the incense of prayer created a cloud as the fragrant smoke of the incense covered the mercy seat on the ark of the covenant. Then God would descend and distill His visible qualities in the midst of the cloud where He would commune with the High Priest. The Presence of God always descended *after* the fragrance of prayer ascended. In our day, an entire kingdom of priests has been authorized and commissioned to minister in God's Presence, offering up unceasing prayer, praise, worship, and intercession for all men.

I have pondered all of these things in the light of Revelation 5:8, which opens a window for us into the operations and functions of the heavenly realm. John tells us there is an altar in Heaven where the angels minister to the Lord continuously. One angel has a censer that must be similar to the fire pan of the Aaronic priests.

And another angel came and stood at the altar, holding a golden censer; and much incense was given to him, that he might add it to the prayers of all the saints upon the golden altar which was before the throne. And the smoke of the incense, with the prayers of the saints, went up before God out of the angel's hand. And the angel took the censer; and he filled it with the fire of the altar and threw it to the earth; and there followed peals of thunder and sounds and flashes of lightning and an earthquake. (Revelation 8:3-5).

The Bible says that the angel took the censer and filled it with fire from the altar mingled with incense. Beside this altar in Heaven, there is also a golden bowl filled with incense. What is incense? Revelation 5:8 tells us this incense, itself, is the prayers of the saints. What is the Lord's response to the fragrance of the incense of our prayers rising before Him? He commands an angel to turn over that bowl and spill the prayers of the saints onto the fire of the altar! Then the angel takes the censor and fills it with fire from the altar and the incense of the prayers of the saints and casts the fire down from Heaven onto the earth.

As we have said before: *What goes up must come down.* When the prayers of the saints rise as incense before the throne of God, they are gathered into a golden bowl and burned again with the fire of the altar in the presence of the Most High God. This illustrates how our prayers are multiplied and savored by God before He responds by sending His fire to the earth as answered prayer. This is the multi-directional dimension of prayer. Remember, what goes up must come down.

God attends to the prayers of the saints.
Believers are vessels that help make a difference
where judgment ends and mercy begins.

Where Will the Judgments Be Released?

The interesting thing is that the Bible doesn't say where on the earth these judgments will be released. Why is that? Before releasing judgment, God always attends first to the golden bowl, the prayers of the saints. He first listens to the priests who are ministering in the tabernacle at the altar of incense, which is the priestly act of intercession. Believers are vessels that help make a difference where judgment ends and mercy begins.

God has chosen to raise up an entire Kingdom of intercessory priests like Abraham (who interceded for Lot and the cities of Sodom and Gomorra), Moses (who stood between God's wrath and the Israelites repeatedly), Job (who interceded for his friends and was himself healed and restored), Esther (the peasant who became queen and risked death to intercede for the salvation of her entire nation), and Daniel (whose intercession for his nation extended beyond his own time into the last days before the final return of the Messiah). Even more remarkable is the fact that God wants us to model our priesthood after the continual ministry of our Great High Priest, Jesus Christ, who "...is able also to save them to the uttermost that come unto God by Him, seeing He ever liveth to make intercession for them" (Heb. 7:25 KJV).

Exposing the Enemy's Lies

Let me say this for the benefit of everyone who has unknowingly bought the enemy's desperate lies about the supposed uselessness of prayer:

Prayer works. Prayer is powerful. Prayer is one of our most deadly and effective weapons for destroying the works of the enemy. Prayer is God's lifeline to the hurting, the wounded, the weak, and the dying. But He expects you and I to throw out His rope of life in the name of His Son, Jesus. Intercession isn't the preoccupation of the zealous few—it is the calling and destiny of the Chosen people, of every blood-washed child of God. If you call Jesus Christ Savior and Lord, then He calls you intercessor and priest, and today He is calling you to your knees.

A few years ago, I was traveling in the middle of the night on a six-hour train trip from Heidelberg to Rosenheim, Germany. I tried to sleep during that trip, but I kept hearing the gentle voice of the Holy Spirit speak to me. I knew that He was speaking to me as an individual, but He was also voicing His burden for the many-membered people to come forth.

I repeatedly heard that dear Dove utter a piercing, relentless plea: "Where are My Daniels? Where are My Esthers? Where are My Deborahs? And where are My Josephs?"

Jesus Christ has made you and I to be kings and priests unto God. Now I declare to you under the same prophetic anointing that inspired Mordecai when he told his young cousin and ward, Esther, "And who knows whether you have not *attained royalty for such a time as this?*" (Esther 4:14b). For such a task as this were you apprehended, and for this purpose He brought you forth.

As a Christ-like one, you also are named deliverer, kinsman redeemer, healer, and restorer of the breach. Will you arise and be one of His radical revolutionaries? Will you say "Yes, Lord!" and be the *answer* to the Great Intercessor's plea?

Endnotes

1. *Merriam-Webster's Collegiate Dictionary, 10th Edition* (Springfield, Massachusetts: Merriam-Webster, Incorporated, 1994), 609.

Chapter 4

Restoring the Art
of Pleading Your Case

"It is the habit of faith, when she is praying, to use pleas. Mere prayer sayers, who do not pray at all, forget to argue with God; but those who would prevail bring forth their reasons and their strong arguments...."

Charles H. Spurgeon

Unthinkable! How could you presume to argue with God? It is not presumption to obey the Word of God, nor is it presumption to remind God of His mighty works and unmatched power. God is pleased each and every time we come before His throne as we are whispering, reciting, declaring, and pleading for the speedy fulfillment of His unfailing promises in Jesus' name. He is glorified when His children humbly urge and entreat Him to rise in His power on behalf of those in need—when they recite the countless ways He has delivered in the past, is redeeming in the present, and will overcome in the days to come.

Presumption presumes to act on authority that it does not have or has not been given: Obedience only acts on the authority of another or upon the authority that it has been given by a higher authority. We have been given incredible "royal court" privileges and authority by our Lord, Jesus Christ. He has personally made each of us priests and kings with right of entry to the very throne of God. Even a casual glance at the instructions of Jesus concerning the prevailing prayer of the persistent widow who pestered the unrighteous judge to take action in Luke 18:1-8 should be a warning that there is more to this "pleading prayer" than most people believe.

> ... *"Even though I do not fear God nor respect man, yet because this widow bothers me, I will give her legal protection, lest by continually coming she wear me out." And the Lord said, "Hear what the unrighteous judge said; now* **shall not God bring about justice for His elect, who cry to Him day and night,** *and will He delay long over them? I tell you that He will bring about justice for them speedily. However, when the Son of Man comes, will He find faith on the earth?"* (Luke 18:4b-8)

Isaiah, the prophet, battled with an unrepentant and even defiant nation of Israelites who refused to acknowledge sin or abandon its idols even in the face of defeat, bondage, and literal slavery to other nations. Then God issued a challenge to His creation through the prophet that reveals the heart of God toward us— even when we are in sin and trying to justify our rebellion.

> *Put Me in* **remembrance:** *let us* **plead** *together:* **declare** *thou, that thou mayest be justified* (Isaiah 43:26 KJV).

> *Put Me in* **remembrance;** *let us* **argue** *our case together,* **State** *your cause, that you may be proved right* (Isaiah 43:26 NAS).

> Oh, **remind** *Me of this promise of forgiveness, for we must* **talk** *about your sins.* **Plead** *your case for My forgiving you* (Isaiah 43:26 TLB).

This verse reveals the "broad shoulders of God," who is so powerful and confident that He can "afford" to listen the arguments of mankind—even those of angry or disillusioned people who often step far beyond the bounds of wisdom in their complaints to God. He especially delights in the humble but confident prayers of His kings and priests who come to His court in the name and company of His Son, Jesus Christ, approaching Him on the basis of His Word.

Defining the Terms

This clear biblical precedent establishes the fact that we have God's permission and invitation to plead our case and make appeals in the courts of Heaven before our great Judge and God. The dictionary definition of *plead* is "1: to argue a case or cause in a court of law; 2: to make an allegation in an action or other legal proceeding," and a definition for *plea* is "an earnest entreaty."[1]

The Hebrew word translated as "plead" in Isaiah's declaration is *shaphat*. It means "to judge, to pronounce sentence, to vindicate, to punish, or to litigate.[2] The Hebrew word translated as "declare" or "state your cause" is *caphar*, which means "to score with a mark as a tally or record, to inscribe, and also to enumerate; to recount, to number."[3]

These definitions taken together paint a clear picture of a judicial setting described in purely judicial terminology: to argue the case as in a court of law, to pronounce sentence, to punish to litigate. This reinforces my conviction that for us to succeed as intercessors, we must have a revelation of God Almighty as the Judge of all flesh. We are privileged to "practice before the bar" under the authority and invitation of our Judge Advocate, Jesus Christ.

Assisting the Advocate

At our new birth, He was our defense attorney. As intercessors of the Lamb, we serve as assistant advocates of the Kingdom, charged with defending the King's people and prosecuting the King's enemies in the spirit realm (the adversary and his rebellious followers). Each time we come before the "bench" of the Judge of all, our Chief Advocate comes alongside and takes us by the arm to formally present us before the Judge and enumerate the legal credentials that He has delegated to us. We literally "practice before the bar" as assistant advocates sent from His high office as First Born, the Lamb of God, Chief Intercessor, and Chief Advocate of the redeemed.

The writer of Hebrews carefully painted a picture to contrast the difference between man's approach to the Judge before the cross and after the cross. The difference is absolutely crucial:

> *For you have not come to a mountain that may be touched and to a blazing fire, and to darkness and gloom and whirlwind, and to the blast of a trumpet and the sound of words which sound was such that those who heard begged that no further word should be spoken to them. For they could not bear the command, "If even a beast touches the mountain, it will be stoned." And so terrible was the sight, that Moses said, "I am full of fear and trembling"* (Hebrews 12:18-21).

> **As intercessors of the Lamb, we serve as
> assistant advocates of the Kingdom, charged
> with defending the King's people and prosecuting
> the King's enemies in the spirit realm (the
> adversary and his rebellious followers).**

Compare the Old Covenant picture of fear and dread with our place of entry under the New Covenant of the blood of the Lamb:

> *But you have come to Mount Zion and to the city of the living God, the heavenly Jerusalem, and to myriads of angels, to the general assembly and church of the first-born who are enrolled in heaven, and to God, the Judge of all, and to the spirits of righteous men made perfect, and to Jesus, the mediator of a new covenant, and to the sprinkled blood, which speaks better than the blood of Abel* (Hebrews 12:22-24).

The Book of Hebrews describes the dwelling place of God and the beings who dwell there with Him. We are reassured as we realize that when we step before the bench of this Judge, we will be in the company of the worshiping angels and familiar people like Moses; Aaron; Hurr; Isaiah; Deborah; Paul; Barnabus; Simon of Cyrene; Mary the mother of Jesus; Peter the fisherman-made-apostle; Corrie ten-Boom; Teresa of Avila; Paul Billheimer; C.S. Lewis; Nikolaus Ludwig von Zinzendorf; and the Wesley brothers. Do you sense that you would be at home in this place?

Best of all, as we come before the Judge of all to plead our intercessory case, we come to the Advocate, the Merciful One, Jesus Christ the mediator, whose sprinkled blood continually cries out, "Mercy" before the Judge (while the blood of Abel could only cry, "Vengeance!").

When you persistently bring your pleas before the Judge of all in the courtroom of Heaven, the Lord looks upon it as faith. The process of presenting your case and arguments pleases God, and it also helps you understand the need more completely. It moves you in compassion, strengthens your determination, and arms you with a greater depth of holy hunger.

In the first chapter of Isaiah's prophetic book, God declares, "Come now, and let us reason together..." (Is. 1:18). This is an invitation to a court hearing where God is pleased to hear our requests, petitions, and pleas. Job openly longed for such a place:

> *Oh that I knew where I might find Him, that I might come to His seat! I would present my case before Him and fill my mouth with arguments. I would learn the words which He would answer, and perceive what He would say to me* (Job 23:3-5).

I have received a great deal of inspiration and instruction from Wesley Duewel book entitled, *Mighty Prevailing Prayer.* He quotes Charles Spurgeon's comments on intercession in his book: "It is the habit of faith, when she is praying, to use pleas. Mere prayer sayers, who do not pray at all, forget to argue with God; but those who would prevail bring forth their reasons and their strong arguments ... Faith's act of wrestling is to plead with God and say with holy boldness, 'Let it be thus and thus for these reasons.' " Spurgeon preached, "The man who has his mouth full of arguments in prayers shall soon have his mouth full of benedictions in answered prayer."[4] Wesley Duewel outlines a blueprint for reciting or case before God:

> "This holy argumentation with God is not done in a negative, complaining spirit. It is the expression not of a critical heart but of a heart burning with love for God, for His name, and for His glory. This holy debate with God is a passionate presentation to God of the many reasons why it will be in harmony with His nature, His righteous government, and the history of His holy intervention on behalf of His people.
>
> "You do not plead like a negative, legal adversary in the presence of God the holy judge. Rather, you plead in the form of a well-prepared brief, prepared by a legal advocate in behalf of a need and for the welfare of the kingdom. At times you are, as it were, petitioning God's court for an injunction against satan to stop his harassment. The Holy Spirit guides you in the preparation and wording of your prayer argument."[5]

Doing Your Homework!

Effective intercession begins with knowledge and understanding. Do your homework so you will know God's promises. Understand why the promises haven't been fulfilled in specific situations (when possible). Know why society or a particular group has failed. Understand every condition God requires before His various promises are fulfilled. Then commune with Jesus and get His heart on the matter. Let the Holy Spirit be your guide as you present holy argumentation before the righteous Judge of all the living. As you enter His presence, remember that many have come here before you. Thousands of years ago, the prophet Jeremiah and Joshua each ventured to this place of intercession:

Although our iniquities testify against us, O Lord, act for Thy name's sake!... Do not despise us, for Thine own name's sake; Do not disgrace the throne of Thy glory; Remember and do not annul Thy covenant with us (Jeremiah 14:7, 21).

Joshua pleaded with God to help Israel asking, "What will You do for Your own namesake?" (Joshua 7:9b)

In the Footsteps of Abraham

One of the first great intercessors in the Bible was Abraham, and his most famous intercessory prayer was for one of the most sinful places in the ancient world! Sodom and Gomorra have become synonymous with sin, sexual debauchery, and sodomy, yet the great Patriarch of Israel, the "father of faith" interceded passionately that those twin cities of sin be spared! I believe it was this kind of compassion that led God to say, "Shall I hide from Abraham what I am about to do?" (Gen. 18:17)

> **God quits when man quits. What did you say, Jim? Yes, God quits when man quits!**

When God told Abraham that He planned to destroy Sodom and Gomorra, the patriarch asked God if He planned to destroy the righteous people along with the wicked. Abraham then made the counterproposal, "...wilt Thou indeed sweep it away and not spare the place for the sake of the fifty righteous who are in it?" (Gen. 18:24b). When God agrees to relent if 50 righteous people were found, Abraham persisted to drive the numbers lower, knowing only Lot and his family could possibly qualify. The patriarch whittled the number down to 20, and in verse 32 he reached a pivotal place that is important for us to see. Abraham said, "Oh may the Lord not be angry, and I shall speak only this once; suppose ten are found there?" (Gen. 18:30)

God agrees to Abraham's request, but this passage caused us to wonder, *What if Abraham hadn't stopped at ten?* God definitely showed no signs of being angry with Abraham over his

persistent intercession and pleading on behalf of Sodom and Gomorra. In fact, I believe God liked it. I believe Abraham could
have gone even lower. (But then again I wasn't there and I cer-
tainly don't have all the facts at hand.) However, this incident illustrates one of the fundamental laws governing the relationship
between God and man: God quits when man quits. What did you
say, Jim? Yes, God quits when man quits!

Biblical Definitions

There are four biblical definitions of an intercessor that help
paint a clear picture of our general calling as priestly intercessors
and will bring everything else we study into proper perspective.

An Intercessor Is One Who:

1. Reminds the Lord of promises and appointments not yet
   met and fulfilled.

*On your walls, O Jerusalem, I have appointed watchmen;
All day and all night they will never keep silent. You who
remind the Lord, take no rest for yourselves; and give
Him no rest until He establishes and makes Jerusalem a
praise in the earth* (Isaiah 62:6-7).

2. Takes up the case of justice before God on behalf of
   another.

*Yes, truth is lacking; and he who turns aside from evil
makes himself a prey. Now the Lord saw, and it was dis-
pleasing in His sight that there was no justice. And He saw
that there was no man, and was astonished that there was
no one to intercede* (Isaiah 59:15-16a).

3. Makes up the hedge, and builds up the wall of protection
   in time of battle.

*O Israel, your prophets have been like foxes among ruins.
You have **not** gone up into the breaches, nor did you build
the wall around the house of Israel to stand in the battle on
the day of the Lord* (Ezekiel 13:4-5).

4. Stands in the gap between God's righteous judgment which is due and the need for mercy on the people's behalf.

*"And I searched for a man among them who should **build up the wall and stand in the gap** before Me for the land, that I should not destroy it; but I found no one. Thus I have poured out My indignation on them; I have consumed them with the fire of My wrath; their way I have brought upon their heads,"* declares the Lord God (Ezekiel 22:30-31).

Responding to His Promises

Priestly intercessors deal with two kinds of promises: the promises recorded in the Word of God which are yet to be fulfilled or are ongoing promises available to every believer by faith; and prophetic promises given to us in our day which are true, but are yet to be fulfilled (see First Tim. 1:18-19).

God tells us in the Book of Jeremiah that He is watching over His Word to perform it (see Jer. 1:12). That means the most valid and effective way to present our case before God is to rehearse and respectfully remind Him of His unchanging Word. When we rehearse a promise from our faithful God, *He requires Himself* to watch over that Word to perform it. But this entreaty only can be done with the purest of motives from hearts that are clean before God. Even then, we are only authorized to "argue" or present our case for those things and petitions which (1) are in accordance with God's will; (2) extend His Kingdom; and (3) glorify His name.

Wesley Duewel lists seven bases of appeal for intercessory prayer in his book, *Mighty Prevailing Prayer*. These points provide a powerful platform of knowledge for anointed and effective intercession. It is not enough to get inspired and to have sincerity when we pray. We need to understand our God-given rights and privileges, and we need to understand our limitations and boundaries. That way, we can stand before the Judge in confidence. We will know that we are not merely trying to "twist the arm of God" to get Him to do something that He does not want to do. Quite to the contrary, we are called to ask Him to do what He wants to do for us! What a deal!

A. Plead the Honor and Glory of God's Name

1. God saved Israel at the Red Sea for His name sake "...that He might make His power known" (Ps. 106:8).
2. Samuel prayed for the sake of God's own name (see 2 Sam. 7:26).
3. David, knowing the God-given responsibility kingship placed upon him, prayed for guidance (Ps. 23:3; 31:3), and for help (Ps. 109:21; 143:11), and for God's name sake.
4. Asaph prayed for God to help Israel " ...for the glory of Your holy name" (Ps. 79:9a).

B. Plead God's Relationships to Us

1. God is our *Creator* and we are the work of His hands (Job 10:3,8-9;14:15; Ps. 119:73).
2. God is our *Helper* (Ps. 33:20; 40:17; 63:7), our ever-present help (Ps. 46:1).
3. God is our *Redeemer* (Ps. 19:14; Is. 41:14; 54:5). He will have compassion on us because He is our Redeemer (Is. 54:8; 63:16).
4. God is our *Father* (Is. 64:8, Mal. 3:17, Rom. 8:15), and we are privileged to cry out as children to their father, "Abba [Daddy], Father" (Rom. 8:15; Gal. 4:6).

Since He is our Creator, Helper, Redeemer, and Father, we can make our plea to Him for protection and provision for all He has created and redeemed.

C. Plead God's Attributes

1. Plead God's *righteousness* as Nehemiah did (Neh. 9:33). Christ speeds the cause of the righteous (Is. 16:5).
2. Plead on the basis of God's *faithfulness* as Ethan did in Psalm 89, where he makes his holy plea according to God's faithfulness six times.

3. Plead on the basis of His *mercy and love*. Join Moses (Deut. 9:18), David (Ps. 4:1, 27:7, 30:10; 86:6, 15-16), and Daniel and the three Hebrew children (Dan. 2:18).
4. Charles Spurgeon said, "We shall find every attribute of God Most High to be, as it were, a great battering ram with which we may open the gates of heaven."

D. Plead the Sorrows and Needs of God's People
1. David was one who took upon himself the suffering of his people. He even wept for the suffering of his enemies (Ps. 35:11-13). Nehemiah, and Daniel in particular, also used this plea greatly as they vicariously identified themselves with the sufferings of the people.
2. Jeremiah, perhaps more than others, used this form of plea as he prevailed for his people. He pleads for God to look and see the sufferings (Lam. 2:20), and to remember, look, and see (Lam. 5:1). In great detail he lists for God all the sufferings of the people. He does not try to justify his people, for he knows how deserving they are of God

Let me give you a contemporary example: I have ministered in the Caribbean nation of Haiti 14 different times. It is the poorest country in the western hemisphere, and it is one of the poorest nations in the world. The adult per capita income before the recent food embargo was $300 a year. Among adult males in the capital city of Port Au Prince, the unemployment rate has been 80 percent! Disease is rampant. If you go into nearby suburbs like the city of Solle, conditions are horrendous with no sanitation facilities or bathrooms. (I didn't even see an outhouse when I walked the streets at Solle.) In the 1800s, Haiti was called "the pearl of the Antilles," and Port Au Prince was supposedly named for the Prince of Peace. But the people so desperately wanted their independence from the domination of France that they dedicated the nation to satan believing he would give them power to be free.

Well, they got their freedom from France, but they received enslavement to the dark powers driving their voodoo religion. At the same time, these are some of the most lovely people I have ever met. My heart aches to again see the many wonderful God-fearing believers I've met in that nation. The indigenous church is arising, and my prayer for this nation that was dedicated to darkness is this: "Father, bring these precious people to repentance, and break the bondage of satan that binds them. Restore them into their ancient godly heritage and make them once again the pearl of the Antilles. Let God arise and His enemies be scattered!"

E. Plead the Past Answers to Prayer

1. David reminded God of His past mercy: "Thou hast been my help..." (Ps. 27:9b). "O God, Thou hast taught me... even when I am old and gray, O God do not forsake me" (Ps. 71:17-18a). A number of psalms remind God and the people in detail of His past mercies (see Ps. 78; 85:1-7; 105; 106; and 136).

2. Like David, you can present pleading arguments for new mercies on the basis of the history of all He previously has done. But the task is yet unfinished. God has invested too much to stop now. Plead for God's continuing mercy and power to be renewed to bring the final victory.

3. What has God done for you? How have your prayers been answered in the past? Just begin to praise and thank the Lord for the answers of the past, and renewed faith will arise within you for your plea saying of today.

F. Plead the Word and the Promises of God

1. David cried to God reverently, humbly, and lovingly, yet with holy insistence. He pressed for fulfillment of God's promise, "...Do as Thou hast spoken...and let Thy name be established and magnified forever...therefore Thy servant hath found courage to pray before Thee. And now, O Lord, Thou art God and hast promised this good thing to Thy servant" (1 Chron. 17:23-26).

2. Solomon prayed the same way. He held God to the promises that He had made to David, his father: "…O Lord,
the God of Israel, there is no god like Thee in heaven or
on earth, keeping covenant and showing lovingkindness
to Thy servants who walk before Thee with all their
heart; who has kept with Thy servant David, my father,
that which Thou hast promised him; indeed, Thou hast
spoken with Thy mouth, and hast fulfilled it with Thy
hand, as it is this day. Now therefore, O Lord, the God of
Israel, keep with Thy servant David, my father, that
which Thou hast promised him, saying, 'You shall not
lack a man to sit on the throne of Israel, if only your sons
take heed to their way, to walk in My law as you have
walked before Me.' Now therefore, O Lord, the God of
Israel, let Thy word be confirmed which Thou hast spoken to Thy servant David." (2 Chron. 6:14-17). This was
no mincing of words. God had spoken. Now Solomon in-
sisted that God fulfill His Word.

For 11 years I was a part of the leadership team of what today
is called Metro Christian Fellowship in Kansas City, Missouri. In
that time, I had the awesome privilege of participating in countless numbers of prayer gatherings led under the inspiration of the
senior pastor, Mike Bickle. Meeting by meeting, day by day, and
month by month, Mike and scores of "faceless people" would
take their stand before God and remind Him of His Word. Praying
the prayers of the Bible, turning Scripture portions into intercession, pleading promises of this grand book back to God. This ancient art is intercession in one of its purest forms.

G. Plead the Blood of Jesus
1. Perhaps the greatest, most powerful, most answerable
plea of all is the blood of Jesus. No more prevailing argu-
ment we can bring before God than the sufferings, blood,
and death of His Son. We have no merit of our own. We
do not prevail by techniques or past experience. No

prayer "know-how" prevails. It is only through the blood of Jesus.

> The name of Jesus and the blood of Jesus—
> glory in them, stake your all on them, and use
> them to the glory of God and the routing of
> satan. Let there be a generation of people
> arise that are consumed with this passion,
> with this vision of the blood of Jesus.

2. Bring before the Father the wounds of Jesus. Remind the Father of the agony of Gethsemene. Recall to the Father the strong cries of the Son of God as He prevailed for our world and for our salvation. Remind the Father of earth's darkest hour on Calvary, as the Son triumphed alone for you and me. Shout to Heaven again Christ's triumphant cry, "It is finished!" Plead the cross. Plead His wounds over and over again.

3. Pray until you have the assurance of God's will. Pray until you have been given by the Spirit a vision of what God longs to do, needs to do, and waits to do. Pray until you are gripped by the authority of the name of Jesus. Then plead the blood of Jesus. The name of Jesus and the blood of Jesus—glory in them, stake your all on them, and use them to the glory of God and the routing of satan. Let there be a generation of people arise that are consumed with this passion, with this vision of the blood of Jesus.

The Power of the Blood!

Over the past 20-plus years my wife and I have had the privilege of knowing Mahesh and Bonnie Chavda of All Nations Church in Charlotte, North Carolina. Mahesh has traveled the globe, and through the authentic healing ministry of Jesus Christ, through our dear humble brother, he has seen every healing listed in the New Testament, including the dead being raised.

One time, when Mahesh was ministering in Zaire, Africa, he stood before a multitude of over 100,000 people. The Holy Spirit spoke to him to conduct a mass deliverance service. Mahesh answered back, "But Lord, where are my helpers?"

Our persistent great God responded, "I am thy Helper! Know this—one drop of the blood of My Son, Jesus, is more powerful than all the kingdom of darkness." With this powerful revelation, Mahesh proceeded, and thousands were cleansed, healed, and delivered that day.

Let us join in with evangelist Reinhardt Bonnke as he issues a proclamation for a "blood-washed Africa!" Let us arise and join the prayers of Spurgeon, Moody, Chavda, and others. Let's declare what of the blood of Jesus, our Messiah, has accomplished for us.

Come, Let Us Argue Together

What is the final outcome? What will be the score at the end of such a day? Our result is spelled out by the prophet Isaiah who declared by God's Spirit: "Put Me in remembrance; let us argue our case together. State your cause, *that you may be proved right*" (Is. 43:26).[6]

There is a Kingdom to expand and extend. There are blood-washed believers to uplift and protect in prayer. There are millions of lost and dying people desperately in need of the Savior. There are evil forces to bind and dispel through the weapons of divine warfare. It is time to prepare a court brief, to devise arguments of divine value and merit based on the ancient promises of our Eternal God. Are you prepared to approach the bench of the Most High as an advocate of His people, His purposes, and His glory? Gather your case, check your heart, and fall to your knees. The court of the Righteous Judge is always convened and ready to hear your pleas. What case are you ready to bring?

(I strongly recommend to you Wesley Duewel's excellent book, *Mighty Prevailing Prayer*. Leonard Ravenhill called it "the encyclopedia on prayer." I believe it. Much of what I have presented to you on the subject of "pleading your case" was inspired by (or derived) from the material in *Mighty Prevailing Prayer*.)

Endnotes

1. Merriam-Webster's Collegiate Dictionary, 10th Edition, 893.

2. James Strong, *Strong's Exhaustive Concordance of the Bible* (Peabody, Massachusetts: Hendrickson Publishers, n.d.), **lead** (#5608).

3. Strong's, **declare** (#5608).

4. Wesley Duewel, *Mighty Prevailing Prayer* (Grand Rapids: Francis Asbury Press, 1990).

5. Duewel, *Mighty Prevailing*.

6. Duewel, *Mighty Prevailing*.

Chapter 5

Restoring the Watch of the Lord

"I will restore the ancient tools of the Watch of the Lord that have been used and will be used again to change the expression of Christianity across the face of the earth."

June, 1991

This prophetic word came to me in the middle of the night on the Kansas plains. I had brought 30 people with me to that remote area for a prayer retreat at a country lodge. We were praying around the clock in prayer teams for "hour watches" or prayer periods, modeled after military sentry patterns. Our focus was not on fellowship or even a prayer list; we were there to seek God's face. As usual, I had chosen the 2:00-to-3:00 a.m. time slot because the Lord had been waking me up at that time virtually two or three times a week for more than a decade.

As I waited on the Lord, I suddenly saw a picture of an old farm implement, the kind of plow that used to be drawn by horses. When I asked the Lord what it was, the Holy Spirit said, "These are the ancient tools." When I asked what these were, the response was immediate: "The *Watch of the Lord* is the ancient tool." Now that phrase went deep inside of me and stuck.

As I continued to wait before the Lord in that quiet, far-removed place, I saw the tool again and the Lord said, "I will restore the ancient tool of the Watch of the Lord. It has been used and will be used again to change the expression of Christianity across the face of the earth." It sounded very similar to something the Lord said to my friend, Pastor Mike Bickle, when he was in Cairo, Egypt, in 1982. The Lord spoke to him about a move of the Spirit that was coming. He said, "I will change the understanding and the expression of Christianity across the face of the earth in one generation."

I was already familiar with the concept of "watching in prayer" in the Old and the New Testaments (sorry to say, it is sorely missing from the life of the Church at large). This clear word of the Lord given under the starry skies of Kansas lit a fire under me that ultimately propelled me into the borderland of ancient Saxony, the ancient site of the Moravian prayer watch at Herrnhut that I described earlier.

Few English-speaking people use the term, "Watch of the Lord," in our day. Books on prayer seldom discuss it. Yet the importance of the Watch of the Lord, or of watching in prayer, is very important to the plans and order of God. Jesus commanded us to "watch" with Him in several gospel accounts, particularly in the time called "the last days."

Much has been taught about "the last days" by teachers in Evangelical and Pentecostal/Charismatic circles. But exceptionally little has been taught about the *biblical response* of God's people to the last days. I made a comparative study of the verbs Jesus used in Matthew 24, Mark 13, and Luke 21, where He described how we should respond when we see earthquakes, famines, wars and rumors of wars, and so on. Here is a summary of these responses:

See Matthew 24 (NIV):
   "Watch out that no one deceive you" (verse 4).
   "See to it that you are not alarmed" (verse 6).

"Stand firm to the end" (verse 13).
"Keep watch" (verse 42).

See Mark 13:

"Watch out that no one deceives you" (verse 5).
"Do not be alarmed" (verse 7).
"Be on your guard" (verse 9).
"Do not worry" (verse 11).
"Stand firm" (verse 13).
"Be on your guard" (verse 23).
"Be on your guard. Be alert" (verse 33).
"Keep watch" (verse 35).
"Watch out" (verse 37).

See Luke 21:

"Watch out that you are not deceived" (verse 8).
"Do not be frightened" (verse 9).
"Stand firm" (verse 19).
"Stand up and lift up your heads" (verse 28).
"Be careful" (verse 34).
"Be always on the watch and pray" (verse 36).

All of these statements can be summarized in three main phrases: "Do not be afraid" (mentioned four times), "Stand firm" (mentioned four times), and "Watch." Jesus used this key word, "watch," 11 times—almost three times more than any other admonition! Once again, you can hear His voice saying to the Church, "The key I give you is 'watch.' " In Matthew 18:19-20, He gave us the keys of the kingdom, and they have to do with prayer:

Again I say to you, that if two of you agree on earth about anything that they may ask, it shall be done for them by My Father who is in heaven. For where two or three have gathered together in My name, there I am in their midst (Matthew 18:19-20).

Jesus wants groups of two or three people to gather in His name and *ask* in symphony or harmony. (The Greek word translated "agree" is *sumphoneo*, or "harmonious.") This is the heart of the "watch of the Lord." I know it's profound, but you don't need a doctorate in theology or linguistics to understand it.

The Greek word for "watch" in these verses is *gregoreuo*, and it means "to be vigilant, wake, to be watchful."[1] A watchman on the wall does many things. He carefully watches what is happening and alerts the community when good ambassadors approach the city. The guardsman then will open the gates and lower the bridge so the ambassadors may enter. A watchman also warns the city far in advance when an enemy approaches. He sounds an alarm to awaken the people because he knows "to forewarn them is to alert and arm them." Then they quickly can rally to take their stand on the wall against the enemy before he wrongfully tries to enter into the city.

Putting Out the Welcome Mat

We are to watch for the good things and good messengers God sends to His people. We are to watch for the gifted ones and the coming of the Lord's Presence. We are to alert the people to roll out the welcome mat, saying, "Come, come, come, come! Angels of healing, you are welcome here. Spirit of the Lord, You are welcome here. Gifts of the Spirit, you are welcome here. Spirit of conviction of sin, righteousness, and judgment come; you are welcome here. Come, come, come, come!" We are to roll out the red carpet to the name and the blood of Jesus, and say, "Come!"

> Little keys unlock big doors. The Moravians
> discovered a key of power in Leviticus 6:13,
> where the Lord says, "Fire shall be kept burning
> continually on the altar; it is not to go out."
> They believed the New Covenant fire on the
> altar was prayer, and they acted on God's
> challenge. The Moravians actually managed
> to change the world with that little key.

We are to watch to see what the Lord is saying and doing. And we are to look at what the enemy's plans could be. Paul warned us not to be ignorant concerning the devil's schemes (see 2 Cor. 2:11).

God wants to tip us off beforehand to cut off, postpone, delay, or even entirely dismantle the works of the enemy and frustrate his plans for evil.

But as watchers on the wall of the Lord, we go far beyond any dictionary definition. God wants us to look into the mirror of His great Word and discern those things that He has said that He wants to do. Then we are to remind Him of those things that He wants to do and is, at the same time, waiting for us to ask Him to do. Why? Because He has given us that little key called the "prayer of agreement."

Little keys unlock big doors. The Moravians discovered a key of power in Leviticus 6:13, where the Lord says, "Fire shall be kept burning continually on the altar; it is not to go out." They believed the New Covenant fire on the altar was prayer, and they acted on God's challenge. The Moravians actually managed to change the world with that little key. Let me quote a brief article by Leslie K. Tarr that describes these remarkable people:

A Prayer Meeting That Lasted 100 Years[2]

"Fact: The Moravian community of Herrnhut in Saxony, in 1727, commenced an around-the-clock 'prayer watch' that continued non-stop for over a hundred years.

"Fact: By 1792, 65 years after the commencement of that prayer vigil, the small Moravian community had sent forth 300 missionaries to the ends of the earth!

"Could it be that there is some relationship between those two facts? Is fervent intercession a basic component in world evangelization? The answer to both questions is surely an unqualified 'yes.'

"The heroic 18th century evangelization thrust of the Moravians has not received the attention it deserves. But even less heralded than their missionary exploits is that one-hundred-year prayer meeting that sustained the fires of evangelism!

"During its first five years of existence, the Herrnhut settle-
ment showed few signs of spiritual power. By the beginning of 1727, the community of about three hundred
people was wracked by dissension and bickering, an unlikely site for revival.

"Zinzendorf and others, however, covenanted to pray and labor for revival. On May 12, revival came. Christians were
aglow with new life and power, and dissension vanished
and unbelievers were converted.

"Looking back to that day and the four glorious months that
followed, Count Zinzendorf later recalled: 'The whole
place represented truly a visible habitation of God among
men.' A spirit of prayer was immediately evident in the
fellowship and continued throughout that 'golden summer
of 1727,' as the Moravians came to designate that period.
In August 27 of that year, twenty-four men and twenty-
four women covenanted to spend one hour each day in
scheduled prayer. Some others also enlisted in the 'hourly
intercession.'

" 'For over 100 years, the members of the Moravian church
all shared in the "hourly intercession." At home and
abroad, on land and sea, this prayer watch ascended un-
ceasingly to the Lord,' stated historian A.J. Lewis.

"*The Memorial Days of the Renewed Church of the Brethren*,
published in 1822, ninety-five years after the decision to
initiate the prayer watch, quaintly describes the move in
one sentence: 'The thought struck some of the brethren
and sisters that it might be well to set apart certain hours
for the purpose of prayer, at which seasons all might be reminded of its excellency and be induced by the promises
annexed to fervent, persevering prayer to pour out their
hearts before the Lord.'

"The journal further sites Old Testament typology as warrant
for the prayer watch: 'The sacred fire was never permitted
to go out on the altar (Leviticus 6:13); so in the congregation is a temple of the loving God, wherein He has His

altar and fire, the intercession of His saints should incessantly rise up to Him.'

"That prayer watch was instituted by a community of believers whose average age was probably thirty. Zinzendorf himself was twenty-seven.

"The prayer vigil by Zinzendorf and the Moravian community sensitized them to attempt the unheard-of-mission to reach others for Christ. Six months after the beginning of the prayer watch, the count suggested to his fellow Moravians the challenge of a bold evangelism aimed at the West Indies, Greenland, Turkey, and Lapland. Some were skeptical, but Zinzendorf persisted. Twenty-six Moravians stepped forward for world missions wherever the Lord led.

"The exploits that followed are surely to be numbered among the high moments of Christian history. Nothing daunted Zinzendorf or his fellow heralds of Jesus Christ—prison, shipwreck, persecution, ridicule, plague, abject poverty, and threats of death. His hymn reflected his conviction:

"Ambassador of Christ, Know ye the way to go?,
It leads unto the jaws of death,
Is strewn with thorns and woe.

"Church historians look to the eighteenth century and marvel at the Great Awakening in England and America, which swept hundreds of thousands into God's Kingdom. John Wesley figured largely in that mighty movement and much attention is centered on him. Is it not possible that we have overlooked the place which that round-the-clock prayer watch had in reaching Wesley and, through him and his associates, in altering the course of history?

"One wonders what would flow from a commitment on the part of twentieth century Christians to institute a 'prayer watch' for world evangelization, specifically, to reach those in Zinzendorf's words, 'For whom no one cared.' "

In the first chapter I briefly described my encounter with the Lord along with other intercessors in the Moravian watch tower at Herrnhut. But the full story is a miraculous tale of one little key after another falling into place until God positioned us in the Spirit to receive His commission and empowerment of prayer. In fact, it was a "little key" that played one of the most prominent roles in that appointment with destiny.

After the Lord spoke to me about the restoration of the "ancient tool" of the Watch of the Lord, the study of the Watch of the Lord became one of the passions of my life. In February of 1993, I took the intercessor team mentioned in the first chapter to the Czech Republic for some intercessory prayer assignments concerning that resurrected nation, but our real mission was to cross the border to Herrnhut in ancient Saxony in East Germany to recover the anointing of the Moravian prayer watch.

Keys of Revelation

As we prepared in prayer in advance of the trip, the Lord gave me several keys in the Spirit. I didn't know what they meant at the time, but I wrote them down and watched and waited. The Holy Spirit said, "You are going to find a man named Christian Winter, and he has a key." (I had never met this man or heard of him before.) The Lord also mentioned the number "37." In the days that followed, the Lord led us to Ezekiel 37 (which describes the valley of dead men's bones that God resurrected into a mighty army) and to Revelation 3:7 (where the Word speaks of "the key of David").

When we first arrived in Herrnhut, our team didn't do the usual tourist things. We didn't go to museums or famous churches, look at the sights, or go shopping. We were told to go to a certain place and meet a certain man who would direct us to our housing. We also learned that visitors were allowed to go up into the Herrnhut watchtower on occasion, but you had to have a key enter it. As it turned out, the man we were sent to who took us to our place of lodging was the unofficial steward of the Moravian tower lived in Herrnhut. *His name was Christian Winter!* Was this an accident? A coincidence? There's more.

Christian Winter eagerly handed me the key to the Moravian watchtower when I explained our mission. But God had more in mind. I didn't know it, but this gentleman carried in his heart a divine promise that the Watch of the Lord would be restored! I felt led to deliver an expression to this stranger, someone I'd known for a matter of moments: "The Lord is restoring the ancient Watch of the Lord for which many have waited so long! You have faithfully held the key. Now the Lord will unlock the door and restore the ancient fire."

When Christian Winter looked up, he said, "You are the third man who has spoken this very same word to me."

Our prayer team spent hours in prayer in seclusion before venturing out to the Moravian prayer tower. On February 18, we walked together through the narrow streets of Herrnhut toward the cemetery the Moravians called "God's Acre." We thought that we were just going to pass through the cemetery to reach the tower, and we saw the graves of famous Moravian leaders such as Count Zinzendorf and Anna and David Nitschmann, along with those of many of the missionaries who sold themselves into slavery to take the gospel into closed nations and cultures.

As we began walking through the cemetery, there was a sobering sense that there was something—some anointing or power—that these departed saints had walked in. But this anointing seemed to be dead or long departed. I again was reminded of the Lord's word about "37," and how the Lord had led us earlier to the riveting prophecy in Ezekiel 37 concerning the valley of dead men's bones that were resurrected into a mighty army of God.

Valley of Dry Bones

We felt that we needed to just sit down and wait on the Lord for some reason. We knew the Spirit of God wanted us to pray, to deal with something in some way before we went on. So we all sat down in the middle of the cemetery and continued to wait. I know this is sounds bizarre, but I happened to glance down at the grave marker by which I had made my seat and felt a thrill of the Spirit run through my body—I was sitting on the gravestone of

Christian David, the man Count von Zinzendorf called "the Moravian Moses." He founded the community in 1722 and led 10 different groups of refugee brethren to the lands the Count donated to the tiny Christian community. Now Christian David's tombstone was not one of the major marked tombstones. Again, was this an accident? A coincidence? Although reason could not explain these things, I could not flatly deny the possibility of coincidence at this point. I couldn't help but remember that "little keys open big doors."

As I noted earlier, I sensed that like Ezekiel of old, we were again sitting in a valley of dry bones and that God was again asking us, "Can these bones live again?" Ezekiel identified the dry bones he saw with the broken, fragmented structures of Judaism in his day. We were sitting in that cemetery marking some of the richest prayer, devotion, and missionary endeavor in Church history. When the Lord seemed to ask us anew, "Can these bones live?" we began quietly to confess the sin of the Church. We confessed our prayerlessness through the generations, our own individual sins, and the sin of the current-day Church. And we begin to confess that the Church had dropped the baton of the spirit of prayer. It was a quiet time of confession. There was no "travail" or weeping; there were no so-called "wild manifestations." We were just calmly confessing our sin before the Lord. After a few minutes had passed, we sensed that we "had permission" to proceed to the tower.

The Procession Begins

My wife, Michal Ann, seemed to take the lead at that point along with Susan Shea (now Susan Nichols), a gifted intercessor and dancer. They began to lead us up the hill with prophetic song and procession before the Lord. We weren't consciously superimposing any preconceived ideas or structure on the process—the Lord seemed to be leading us in a spiritual procession of ascents similar to what you see in the Psalms. We had come by the Spirit with a call to restore something ancient to something new, and God was doing the work.

When we reached the tower I took out the key Christian Winter had given me and then it hit me: I was holding the "key of David" that the Spirit had described! The key to the power and effectiveness of the Moravian community was their singlehearted devotion to Jesus Christ and to the Watch of the Lord. No one in modern Church history has wielded this "ancient tool" so effectively or faithfully as Christian David, Count von Zinzendorf, and the Moravian believers.

The "key of David" in my hand looked like a very old skeleton key, but it worked. I opened the door to the spiral staircase leading to the tower and we started climbing. As soon as we reached the top, we began to engage the Spirit through prayer. I've already described the two waves of intercession that swept over us, followed by two strong wind blasts. Yet, it is appropriate to add some details here that I purposely left out in my initial account in the first chapter.

> **The key to the power and effectiveness of the Moravian community was their singlehearted devotion to Jesus Christ and to the Watch of the Lord. No one in modern Church history has wielded this "ancient tool" so effectively or faithfully as Christian David, Count von Zinzendorf, and the Moravian believers.**

It is difficult to exaggerate the ferocity and depth of the burden of the Lord that came over us! My wife and my sister, Barbara, were there with me, along with Sue Kellough, a prophetic intercessor from Indianapolis who is also a respected friend, advisor, and co-laborer with our ministry. Nearby stood James Nichols, a fervent African-American believer whose ancestors came from St. Thomas in the Virgin Islands where they first received the gospel from Moravian missionaries dispatched to serve the slave population of that former Danish colony hundreds of years earlier. We were all crowded together when the first wave of intercession and groaning travail swept over us. Michal Ann remembers the scene well:

"I was just totally overcome by the Holy Spirit in that intense place of prayer. I started crying uncontrollably, and at first it seemed almost inappropriate. The whole group began to stagger under the weight of the burden, but God seemed to use me as an unwitting igniter to ignite a fire that spread through the whole group.

"The intercession that broke out was so intense that people began falling down or doubling over until they fell to the wood floor of the tower. Jim often teaches about being 'possessed for prayer,' and I think the Spirit of God literally began praying through us as we yielded to Him—we were all consumed with this spirit of intercession.

"The best way I know how to say it is that I felt the sorrow and the grief of the Holy Spirit. I could sense His grief and His longing for something holy and powerful to be released. I want to say it was a very emotional, but I felt like I was crying from deep within my soul on behalf of the Holy Ghost. I felt like we were expressing His pain through unspeakable groanings of the Spirit. I can't bring definition to it. All I know is that I was experiencing 'feelings' from His heart to my heart.

"I was so caught up in this intense place of prayer I wasn't thinking of anything else. I don't even remember any particular Scripture coming to my mind. I was just totally focused on this burden that weighed so heavily on me. It was very deep, very concentrated, and very focused. It was a place of vulnerability, and I allowed myself to be so overcome and overwhelmed by God's Spirit that I eagerly yielded to His praying through me. It was like entering the child-birth process. When the time of birth comes, you're exposed, and you're absolutely vulnerable and naked. You can only focus on one thing—bringing forth the baby at its appointed time.

"I remember that some people responded to the weight of the spirit of travail coming on them by falling to the floor or by doubling over. We were pressed together, and it felt kind of cold in the tower at first. However, all that was forgotten once we entered this place of abandoned prayer. We were praying "as one man." It was just like a big fire that got ignited. It just overtook everybody. We were all very focused in that place."

Suddenly, the prayer burden lifted and the wind came. Some of the people from Atlanta were running a tape recorder at the time, and you can actually hear on the tape the wind roaring through the place. The wind and the travail finally died down, but it was only a "breather." The burden of the Lord came on us again. With one voice we began to travail by the Spirit as if we were instruments in the hands of our invisible God. The violent wind once again swept through the Moravian lookout prayer tower. I felt as though the wind came to blow that ancient prayer anointing throughout the world according to the spirit of grace we had just asked for.

A great joy came over us and we started marching around on the watchtower. We were rejoicing in the Lord. Then we felt the Spirit release a quickening faith in us to loose or dispatch the spirit of grace for the Watch of the Lord to into different countries and cities around the world. The Lord was releasing grace for the house of prayer for all nations, and for the Watch of the Lord to be released first in 120 cities across the earth, and then to 3,000 in the pattern of the Book of Acts. God was supernaturally and symbolically fulfilling the prophecy that I'd received on the plains of Kansas two years earlier. The ancient tool of the Watch of the Lord was being released anew on the earth by the winds of God.

Leaders of the Pack Today

There are many others who also carry this torch for unceasing prayer and the Watch of the Lord. Among them are:

1. Our friends and mentors, Mahesh and Bonnie Chavda, who have promoted all-night "Watches of the Lord" to build a "wall of prayer" since 1995, when the Lord showed them that corporate intercession was the missing link between renewal and the coming harvest.

2. Lou Engle, associate pastor at Harvest Rock Church in Pasadena, California, who has carried a burden for "24-hour houses of prayer." He has been praying for revival for more than two decades.

3. Dr. Bill Bright of Campus Crusade for Christ, who in 1994 called for 2 million North Americans to fast and pray for revival for 40 days by the year 2000. This was the fruit of a 40-day fast conducted at the request of the Lord. Dr. Bright's book, *The Coming Revival*, predicts a major worldwide revival will cover the earth by the turn of the century.

4. Wesley Campbell, senior pastor of New Life Vineyard Fellowship in British Columbia, who has called for 100,000 intercessors to fast and pray in 40-day cycles through 1998. This modern-day revivalist warns that "our response [to the call to intercession] now is critical to the magnitude of the outpouring."

5. Mike Bickle, friend, co-worker, and senior pastor of Metro Christian Fellowship in Grandview, Missouri, who has prayed, with his prayer gatherings, three times a day for over a decade for awakening and worldwide revival.

6. Wesley Tullis, a passionate world-class intercessor, who directs the Jericho Center for Prayer and World Evangelization in Colorado Springs, Colorado

5. Tom Hess, who is the founder of the House of Prayer for All Nations on the Mount of Olives in Jerusalem, Israel.

6. Dick Simmons, who is the founder of Men for Nations in our nation's capital. He has been used to release an impartation of the spirit of prayer into my life.

On the Feast of Pentecost when the Holy Spirit was first given, there was the wind, fire, and wine. There was conviction and evangelization, there were signs and wonders, and there were gifts given. Best of all, there was a simple presentation of this glorious man named Christ Jesus. Now on this "second Pentecost" to the Church, we are seeing wine (in the sweet blessings and comfort of the renewal), fire (in the fiery preaching, soul winning, repentance, and call to salvation of the Pensacola revival and elsewhere), and now the wind of the Lord signaling a great harvest. There has never been a greater need for intercession than now.

Endnotes

1. Strong's, watch (Greek #1127).
2. Tarr, "A Prayer Meeting."
3. Wesley Campbell, "100,000 Intercessors!" *Spread the Fire*, (Toronto Airport Christian Fellowship, December 1996) Vol. 2, Issue 6, 15.

Chapter 6

Restoring the Path From Prayer to His Presence

"The greatest hindrance to Christianity today is Christians who do not know how to practice the presence of God."

Rev. Billy Graham

There is to be one primary distinguishing characteristic of the people of God. It is not so much the clothes we wear, the style of our hair, or even the rules by which we conduct ourselves. But there is a "birthmark" of sorts that should set apart every community of true believers, and it should manifest itself in love for one another. Moses reveals this birthmark in a dialogue with God recorded in Exodus 33:14-16:

> *And He said, "My presence shall go with you, and I will give you rest." Then he* [Moses] *said to Him, "If Thy presence does not go with us, do not lead us up from here. For how then can it be known that I have found favor in Thy sight, I and Thy people? Is it not by Thy going with us, so that we, I and Thy people, may be distinguished from all the other people who are upon the face of the earth?"* (Exodus 33:14-16).

This is a key of great power in God's Kingdom. The *Presence of God* is the distinguishing characteristic that proves we have favor with God! Without it, we are as other men. The glory of God is "the manifested Presence of God," the visible evidence that the person of God, Himself, has shown up among us—and that is the greatest thing in life! I believe Moses was crying out to the Lord of Hosts, "Oh, Great One, do not take us up from here unless You go before us. Put *the brilliance of Your great Presence* upon us."

> **"I am going to teach you to release the greatest weapon of spiritual warfare: the brilliance of My great Presence."**

It is no accident that one of the names and titles given Jesus Christ was Immanuel ("God with us"). This chapter was inspired by a word that the Lord planted in me while I was attending a renewal service with Michal Ann in October 1994, at what was then Toronto Airport Vineyard Fellowship. After we were prayed for, we remained still and quiet and waited for the Lord to speak to our hearts. The Holy Spirit began to speak to me, and He said, "I am going to teach you to release the highest weapon of spiritual warfare."

Now that made my spiritual antennas go out! I didn't say anything, but let me tell you I was ready to receive whatever God had for me. At first, the Lord simply told me, "I am going to teach you to release the greatest weapon of spiritual warfare." But finally He added, *"I will teach you to release the brilliance of My great Presence."*

Not long ago, I was ministering on the East Coast when the Spirit of God dropped a sentence into my heart. He said, "I am going to reveal My raw power." I think the Church has gotten too accustomed to "refined sugar." God wants to give us something that's a little more raw and less predictable. C.S. Lewis, in his delightful series of children's books called *The Chronicles of Narnia*, repeatedly warns the central characters that "Aslan the Lion [the Christ figure] is not a *tame lion*." The Church needs to rediscover the truth that the Lion of Judah is *not a tame lion*. God is not *tame*. He cannot be controlled, limited, manipulated, or made "predictable" by mere men who believe they understand everything about God—He is God Almighty, the eternal I AM, the Alpha and Omega, the Ancient of Days. He wants to give us something that is concentrated, condensed, and volatile. He likes to jar us with a "holy jolt" from time to time just to shake us, wake us, and stir us up (but He always does it for our own good).

As I write these words, I am not where I once was, nor am I where I am going to be in the days to come. I'm in yet another season of learning. That is why I want to put a parenthesis around the statement: "I will teach you [because you aren't there yet] to release the brilliance of My great presence."

Being a Spiritual Archaeologist

Sometimes I feel like God has given me a pick and shovel, and a hammer and a brush—then commissioned me as a Holy Ghost archaeologist to search through the ruins of the past for His lost treasures (but I'm not complaining). There is a treasure, a jewel of the Church, that is bright and shining. It is the jewel of God's glory, the manifestation of His glorious Person in our midst. It is His incomparable Presence in all its brilliance. We need to rediscover, recover, and redisplay the family Jewel! I believe God is also saying this to His Church worldwide: "I will teach you to release the brilliance of My great Presence."

I often wear a cross that was given to me as a gift, and it has become very special to me. It is a Moravian cross bearing the symbol of a lamb with a flag of victory. The motto of the Moravians in the 1700s was, "To win for the lamb the rewards for His suffering." As I noted earlier, they launched the "watch of the lord," a continuous prayer vigil that lasted more than a century after the Lord illuminated Count von Zinzendorf's understanding of Leviticus 6:13, which says, " Fire shall be kept burning continually on the altar; it is not to go out."

The Moravians, under the leadership of Count von Zinzendorf, recognized the power in the key of the Lord revealed in

Leviticus 6. So they decided to accept the task of keeping a continual fire of prayer, intercession, and worship burning before the Lord's Presence. I doubt if they realized they would actually keep the fire burning hot and pure for more than 100 years, but they began by making personal commitments to the task.

At first, a total of 48 women and 48 men signed up to pray. Two men prayed together and two women prayed together for a one-hour watch until the next team relieved them. This pattern continued around the clock, day after day and week after week for more than 100 years! The fervent heat generated by the sacrificial fire of their sustained prayer ignited revival fires that launched their pioneering missionary efforts and helped birth the first great awakening through their godly influence on men such as John and Charles Wesley.

All this ties in with the simple revelation that God gave me in the Czech Republic. What I've already mentioned bears repeating again. God asked me, "Have you ever considered the multi-directional dimension of prayer?" Then, He said, *"Remember, what goes up must come down."*

Our prayers ascend to God as sweet-smelling *incense*, and He responds by sending them back down to earth as answered prayers accompanied by His fire. The Old Testament describes in detail the special incense offered to God in the Tabernacle of Moses each day:

> *And you shall put this altar in front of the veil that is near the ark of the testimony, in front of the mercy seat that is over the ark of the testimony, **where I will meet with you**. And Aaron shall burn **fragrant incense** on it; he shall burn it every morning when he trims the lamps. And when Aaron trims the lamps at twilight, he shall burn incense. There shall be **perpetual incense** before the Lord throughout your generations* (Exodus 30:6-8).

> *Then the Lord said to Moses, "Take for yourself spices, stacte and onycha and galbanum, spices with pure frankincense; there shall be an equal part of each. And with it*

*you shall make incense, a perfume, the work of a perfumer,
salted, pure, and holy. And you shall beat some of it very
fine, and put part of it before the testimony in the tent of
meeting, where I shall meet with you; it shall be most holy
to you"* (Exodus 30:34-36).

In the New Testament, we are commanded to "pray without
ceasing" (1 Thess. 5:17). This perfectly parallels God's command
to Moses and Aaron concerning the sweet odor of "perpetual incense" that was to continually waft into the Most Holy Place
from the altar of incense. When I first began to study these verses
in the Book of Exodus, my mind went into gear and I thought:
*Now it's logical that if I can get an understanding of what each
one of these ingredients is, then perhaps it will give me some insight into what God receives as an acceptable sacrifice of prayer.*

What Are the Ingredients of Prayer?

It is extremely interesting that God says these four ingredients
must be mixed in equal proportions. That is a reference to balance. A lot of people (including me) have taught technical proce-
dural steps of prayer labeled with titles like, "The Seven Steps to
Answered Prayer." These sermons are good and mostly valid in
content, but there really aren't seven steps to answered prayer.
The reality which I've discovered is that prayer isn't a technique.
It isn't a thing at all. Neither is prayer a methodology. Prayer is
communion with a Person. Prayer is simply *being with God.*

Prayer is communion with a Person. Prayer is simply *being
with God.*

Despite all of the elaborate rituals and steps of purification
laid down in the Law of Moses, David, the shepherd-king, by-
passed it all to sit in the shadow of the ark of the Covenant on
Mount Zion and commune heart to heart with God (1 Chron.
17:16). He didn't have the bloodlines or credentials of an Aaronic
priest, nor did he belong to the tribe of Levi. Although only the
high priest was allowed in the Most Holy Place, and then only on
one day of the year—David literally sat before the Lord, perhaps

on many occasions. Why? Because prayer is communion, and David had a heart after God's own heart. (This is even more amazing when you realize that all of this happened *before* Jesus died on the cross and removed the veil between God and man. The intensity of David's love overcame the barrier between him and his God.) We have to push past even the correct technical methodologies to get to the heart of God Himself. We must get Him. We must have Him. I know the Old Testament talks about coming into God's courts with praise and His gates with thanksgiving, but the issue is not the technique. The issue is a Person. We're coming to our Father. We're coming to His glorious Son who loves us, who knows us, who gave His life for us. We're coming before the one whom the Book of John says "is in the bosom of the Father" (Jn. 1:18).

More Than a Methodology

I even feel a little hesitant to talk about the four qualities of the incense of prayer, but if we can avoid turning it into a methodology, it will help us in our journey from prayer into His brilliant presence.

1. **Stacte** was a sweet spice. It was found on or near the northern border of Israel and in Syria. It took a full day's journey by foot to reach the trees that oozed forth the resin that was baked until the spice, called *stacte*, emerged. Both the Greek and Hebrew names for this spice mean "to ooze forth or to drop." It was used at times as a metaphor for the emergence of the Word of God or for the act of prophesying. In both cases, it creates the picture of something that has been stored up inside of you oozing or bubbling out from an inner abundance.

When we store up the *logos*, or written Word of God, within our hearts then, when the wind of God breathes upon it, it may become a spoken, revelatory *rhema* word into our lives. The first quality of acceptable incense of prayer is a rich store of the Word of God in our lives which oozes forth upon demand to drop onto other people. Prayer is abiding in the living Word, which is obviously Christ.

It will cost you something to store the Word of God in your life. It will cost you time and a priority shift. It generally will land you in difficult circumstances, but it is worth it. Once you fill your heart with this sweet spice of God's Word, it will ooze forth from every pore of your life and being and permeate your prayers with a sweetness that pleases God and blesses everyone it touches.

2. **Onycha** refers to finely ground aromatic powder produced from a mollusk shell found in the Mediterranean Sea. Although the distance involved to get Onycha was less than that for *stacte*, this powder could be obtained only by making a lengthy trip to the sea to gather a particular type of mollusk or mussel. The mollusk shells were ground into a fine powder and then burned with fire to produce the sweet fragrance so vital to the holy incense.

Our lives should continually release an aroma of fragrant offering unto the Lord. But how does onycha from the Old Testament incense mixture fit into this picture? Have you ever felt like you have been "ground into a pulp" or been broken into little pieces by a trial or circumstance? Have you been "burned" by the thoughtless or deliberate actions of other people? The prayer you offer after enduring these events bears the fragrance of onycha. Scarred prayer warriors reek of onycha. Prayer is a lifestyle of brokenness before God; prayer is communion bathed in the sweet fragrance of a crushed spice called humility and brokenness. David wrote from the depths of brokenness, "The sacrifices of God are a broken spirit; a broken and a contrite heart, O God, Thou wilt not despise" (Ps. 51:17).

3. **Galbanum** is "a yellowish to green or brown aromatic bitter gum resin derived from several Asian plants."[1] The

original Hebrew word, *chelbenah*, meaning "richness or fatness," implies that galbanum comes from the richest or choice part.[2] Galbanum is the oily substance that is used to *hold all the other elements together*.

The overriding conviction that "God is good" will hold your life together and help bring unity among brethren who have different qualities and varying beliefs. Too often we have allowed ourselves to divide into "camps" based on particular areas of truth or emphasis. For example, people of the "Word camp" eat the Word of God. They know the Word, they love the Word, they preach the Word, they proclaim the Word, and they pray the Word—sometimes at the expense of mercy, brokenness, humility, and the character of God. The "brokenness camp" includes many "revival-type people," who at times seem to be in an unspoken competition to see who can get the lowest so God can be the highest. That's all well and good, but it is only one piece of a greater whole. We also need an equal proportion of the extravagance, richness, and fatness of our good God to bind us all together in harmony. To receive anything from God, you "...must believe that He is, and that He is a rewarder of those who seek Him" (Heb. 11:6b). We must believe that He who freely gave His Son will also freely give us all things. We must believe in the richness and the fatness of God.

4. **Frankincense** is "a resin [obtained] from the bark of trees of the genus Boswellia. As the amber resin dries, white dust forms on the drops or tears of frankincense, thus giving rise to its Semitic name. In biblical times most frankincense came either from or via Sheba in southern Arabia."[3] The Hebrew word for frankincense is *lavona*, which literally means "to be white."[4] Perhaps this foreshadowed the righteousness we received when Christ, the scion or branch of David, hung on a tree and shed His blood. By the time the blood of the Lamb dried on the tree and the earth, we were made "the righteousness of God in Christ" by God's grace and love. It is the

blood, shed and applied to us, that cleanses us from all sin. It is through the blood that we are dressed in white and made fit for the Kingdom.

Freshly Made

It is important to remember that the ingredients for the holy incense were purchased fresh each day and mixed in equal proportions. The incense could not be "stored up." Only freshly made incense would do. You and I can't live on the prayers of the past. We can't thrive on the relationship, the intimacy, or the communion that we enjoyed with the Lord *yesterday*.

Day by day, we must make our way into His presence to be renewed, transformed, empowered, and filled with His glory. We have been commissioned to light the fire of prayer and offer sweet-smelling incense created from equal parts of *stacte*, the oozing, bubbling abundance of God's indwelling Word; *onycha*, the sweet crushed spice of inward humility and brokenness; *galbanum*, the unyielding and ingathering faith that God is good; and the purity of *frankincense*, the righteousness of Christ applied and dried upon our hearts in whiteness and holiness unto the Lord.

> **Only freshly made incense would do.**
> **You and I can't live on the prayers of the**
> **past. We can't thrive on the relationship,**
> **the intimacy, or the communion which**
> **we enjoyed with the Lord *yesterday*.**

The priests of old tended the fire of God and carried sweet incense and fire into the Holy of Holies. The priests wore white linen garments adorned with alternating bells and pomegranates on the hem. This speaks of the double blessing of God. The Lord revealed to me as I prayed for my wife that He longs to anoint us with a double blessing, just as Elisha received when Elijah ascended to heaven. God gave the Church nine gifts (signified by the bells signaling that the priests of God are alive and well), and nine fruits of the Spirit (signified by the pomegranates). When we enter His Presence, we are going for the "double blessing" of the fullness of God's character and the fullness of His power.

It was in God's Presence—beyond the veil of separation— that the priests of Aaron approached the ark of the covenant containing symbols of the authority of God (signified by Aaron's rod that budded); the provision of God in the bread of life (marked by pot of the manna God sent from Heaven); the rule and order of God (symbolized by the stone tablets containing the Ten Commandments). All of these could only be approached through mercy, symbolized by the seat of mercy situated between the covering cherubs of God.

This is a beautiful picture of the genuine Church of the redeemed, a Church filled with the sweet-smelling smoke of prayer, praise, worship, and intercession. It is here in the Presence that God says, "I will commune with you there." It is here the we see an abundance of holy gifts, fruit, incense, holiness, mercy, authority, and the sovereign rule of God in the bounds of covenant love. The secret to maturity and purity in the Church is found in the path from prayer to His presence. We *must* get the distinguishing characteristic of the genuine people of God! There was no *natural light* in the Most Holy Place because it wasn't needed or welcome. Just as the Scriptures tell us that God Himself shall be the light to His people, in His Presence we need no natural light (natural or earthbound knowledge or man's wisdom). The only light bathing the Most Holy Place is the light of His brilliant, shining Presence. In our day, we call this light the *shekinah* glory—the manifested glory or Presence of God.

A Dilemma Resolved

Prayer, particularly intercessory prayer, has played a key role in my life and ministry for years. I like a fight. I love to see the works of the devil destroyed. So I have been pondering the various doctrines concerning spiritual warfare, and I've examined my personal experiences in the light of God's Word. I've met with different intercessory leaders around the world to increase my understanding on the controversial issues dealing with principalities, powers, and other things of this nature. God just solved the whole thing for me when He told me, "I'm going to teach you the highest weapon of spiritual warfare—it is releasing the brilliance of My great Presence." Do you want to win? Get soaked in His Presence!

When you get around somebody who smokes, the odor of the smoke permeates your clothing (and lungs) so effectively that other people will think you smoke, too! Why? Because the odor of the smoke gets all over you. When you start spending time with God, the *same thing* happens. In the realm of men, people won't be able to describe it, perhaps, but they will be drawn to the fragrance of mercy, grace, and life that will permeate your being. In the spirit realm, the demons of hell will start thinking that you look a little bit like God—you smell like Him, you glow with a deadly light that they fear. Your presence will remind them of His Presence. The smoke that surrounds the mercy seat of God will be absorbed by your spirit. The atmosphere of Heaven will get into you.

Issues of the Heart

How do you go from prayer to His Presence? It's a heart issue. I'm not going to give you five steps. I can't because I don't know them (although I thought I used to). All I can say is: Lay down your life and learn mercy, and God will meet you to commune with you there.

Hebrews 4:16 tells us, "Let us therefore draw near with confidence to the throne of grace, that we might receive mercy and may find grace to help in time of need." Jesus said, "But go and learn what this means. I desire compassion [mercy KJV] and not sacrifice, for I did not come to call the righteous, but sinners" (Mt. 9:13). God communes with us at the seat of mercy. It doesn't go away; it is the very atmosphere and environment of God's presence.

This gets to the core of what we call religion. Man's religion is judgment pending criticism, legalism, and debate. God does not want us operating out of judgment. He wants us operating out of the seat of mercy.

A man, named Rex Andrews walked with the Lord but he fell away in the 1940s. Then God reached out in His mercy and changed him, and he returned to the Lord. The Presence of God was restored to him in a moment. In 1944, at the height of World War II, God gave this man a revelation through a gift of prophecy of what mercy is. God told him:

> "Mercy is God's supply system for every need everywhere. Mercy is that kindness, compassion, and tenderness, which is a passion to suffer with or participate in another's ills or evils in order to relieve, heal, and restore—to accept another freely and gladly as he is—and to supply the need of the good of life to build up, to bring to peace, and keep in peace. It is to take another into one's heart just as he is, to cherish and nourish him there. Mercy takes another's sins, evils and faults as its own and frees the other by bearing them to God. This is called the glow of love. This is the anointing."

Even though we store up the Word, ask for the cross of brokenness, walk in the reality that God is good and that we are bound together by His extravagance, His richness, and His fatness, and clothe ourselves in the gift of righteousness made available to us through the blood of Jesus—there is something more. When we take this freshly mixed incense, offer it on the fires of fervent prayer, and take it beyond the veil, *there is still one more necessary thing.* We need to have *mercy* built into our lives.

I long to be a person of His presence. I'm not who I was. I'm not who I yet want to be. I long to be a person of His Presence— one who spends time with Him and then releases the brilliance of His great Presence to the world around me. The Lord looking for such a people who will simply come and *be with Him.* He wants a nation of kings and priests who diligently will go from prayer to

His Presence and bear the distinguishing characteristic of His people—*God with us.*

I believe that the Church has been corporately ministering at the altar of incense for the last 15 years, but, in one sense, has never gone inside where His Presence abides. Now, it is as though we are crossing over the threshold and through the veil into the place of His manifested Presence. It is a new beginning, a fresh start. That's why there's a new wind blowing across the earth, a wind called renewal, revival—and a hunger for a great awakening to come.

I'm not who I was. I'm not who I yet want to be. I long to be a person of His Presence— one who spends time with Him and then releases the brilliance of His great Presence to the world around me.

What is the Lord requiring of us? He is calling us to be with Him. It's time to cross over, to abide in His Presence: "Come, come, come!" says the Lord. "Come, come, come before Me."

Prayer is not a technique. Prayer is not a methodology. Prayer is not a matter of "steps one, two, and three." It is our coming to a Person and being saturated with the communion of His great and glorious Presence. God is restoring the fire on the altar in His Church today. During the last 15 to 20 years, renewed fires of prayer have circled the earth. That is marvelous! It is the first time that these renewed fires have burst forth to this degree on a global scale. But, I want to tell you that God is at the brink of taking us even deeper—because this is not a matter of technique or know-how. It doesn't hinge on what seminars we go to or whose tape sets or videos we buy. The Church is learning anew what the Moravians and others discovered almost half a millennium ago. The greatest thing in life is to be able to touch the heart of God and have His heart touch you. It is time to enter and bask in His brilliant Presence.

Endnotes

1. Merriam-Websters Collegiate Dictionary, 10th Edition (Springfield, Massachusetts: Merriam-Webster, Incorporated, 1994), 477.

2. Strong's, **galbanum** (#2464).

3. R. Laird Harris, Gleason L. Archer, Jr., Bruce K. Waltke, eds. *Theological Wordbook of the Old Testament Vol. 1* (Chicago: Moody Press, 1980), *lebona*, **frankincense** (#1074.4), 468.

4. Strong's, **frankincense** (#3828).

Chapter 7

Restoring the House of Prayer for All Nations

Jesus said, "Is it not written, 'My house shall be called a house of prayer for all the nations'?" (See Mk. 11:17.)

I am grateful to be alive today. We're seeing the Son of God enter His Father's house again with fiery zeal to turn the tables on the agendas of wayward men. Once again the Lamb of God has stormed into His Papa's house with the zeal of the Lord of Hosts eating Him up. He isn't content just to turn over our tables of religious pomp and circumstance and man-pleasing programs. He is moving on to the cages that we've constructed with our rigid religion to confine and control the Dove of God, the Holy Spirit! I can almost hear Him say, "My Dove, men have thought to keep You in a cage, but I am going to rattle this cage once again and send You forth. For where the Spirit of the Lord is, there is liberty."

I can almost imagine the scene in the temple of Herod, when a commotion arose on one side as the Spirit of God moved upon the children in the temple. I can imagine the Spirit causing even the smallest little children to prophesy and sing praises in ecstasy. Almost out loud, I can hear the disapproving murmurs of the religious crowd, "It hasn't been seen this way before, and we don't like it."

The zeal of the Lord of Hosts is loose in the land. The power and anointing in the Church is escalating as God releases the zeal of the Father's house upon His people. It brings holy boldness and an unquenchable spirit of prayer. It stems from the holy jealousy of God who is declaring in a loud voice, "I'm coming to take over My house and to claim My house for My own." In the Spirit, I can hear Jesus declare to this generation of believers:

"You have made My house into a den of thieves, but I say that My Father's house shall be called **a house of prayer for all the nations.** As it was in the last days of My earthly ministry, so shall it be in the last days of My ministry in the earth by the power of the Holy Spirit. Zeal for My Father's house will come upon you, and there will be a declaration that shall go forth in the latter days.

"There will be an understanding that will go forth: The Father's house is not first the house of preaching. The Father's house is not first the house of sacraments. The Father's house is not first a house of fellowship or supernatural gifts. My house shall have many of these things, but My Father's house shall be known first as a house of prayer for all nations—of people being built together, holy, on fire, compassionate; of living stones being brought together as they seek My face. And there will be a smoke that shall come forth from these living stones being built together. And the smoke signal shall rise up to the highest heaven and will be received. This smoke is called the incense of prayer." (See Psalm 69:9 and John 2:17.)

In Mark 11:17, Jesus said, "...Is it not written, '**My house shall be called a house of prayer for all the nations**'? But you have made it a **robbers' den.**" Jesus Christ personally cleansed the temple of merchandisers who had desecrated and defiled His Father's "house of prayer." All four gospels carefully record this demonstration of the jealousy of God (Mt. 21:12-13; Mk. 11:15-17, Lk. 19:45, Jn. 2:14). John's account says that Jesus personally fashioned a whip with cords for the task. The Lord condemned the actions of men by saying in effect, "You changed My Father's house and made it into something that it should never become! You have made it into a den of thievery." Christ quoted from the scroll of Isaiah before He declared that the will, the purpose, and the heart of the Father had been violated (Is. 56:7).

He said the house of God was to be marked for prayer for all nations. The Greek word for nations is *ethnos*. God intended for His "house of prayer" to take a worldwide "redemptive intercessory posture" that extends far beyond Israel. Every believer in this royal priesthood is called to worship, praise, prayer, and intercession. Although prayer or worship is never specifically listed among the spiritual grace gifts, *charisma* in the Greek, like the gift of faith or the gift of discerning of spirits, we do find an anointing upon the Levitical priesthood of the Old Testament that foreshadows the anointing on the new order of priests under the blood. Instead of one small family being set aside to be worshipers, God marked an entire nation of faith with blood as His own.

Where Is Prayer on the Gift List?

Ephesians chapter four describes the leadership gifts (*doma* in the Greek) of apostles, prophets, evangelists, pastors and teachers, but prayer and worship specifically are not listed there either. Yet after quizzing our Father many times, I have come to the strong conviction that God purposefully omitted them. Why? Because as New Testament believers before God the Father and His Christ, we are each called before the throne of God to offer continual sacrifices of worship, praise, and prayer (including intercession).

Worship is the act and attitude of wholeheartedly giving yourself to God with all of your spirit, soul, and body. The Greek word translated as "worship" is *proskuneo*. It means "to kiss, like a dog licking his master's hand; to prostrate oneself in homage, reverence, and adoration (see Mt. 4:10). Jesus told the Samaritan woman at the well that God was looking for those who would worship Him in spirit and in truth (Jn. 4:23).

Intercession means to make a request to a superior. Prayer is our means of asking our loving Father God for His intervention

on our behalf night and day (Lk. 11:13). Prayer is our key to release His blessings to one another for salvation, healing, anointing, and every other personal and corporate need. We are to offer
prayers on behalf of people, cities, churches, nations, family groups,
and the thousands of tribes in the earth. According to Revelation
chapters 5 and 8, worship and prayer are to come together as a seam-
less garment worn by the priests of God—joined, united, and wed
together. God is seeking people who will worship *and* pray! He told
Ezekiel that He had found no one who would stand in the gap and
intercede, and He was appalled (see Ezekiel 22:30).

A Heart Bowed Down

Expressions of prayer and worship continually appear together throughout the New Testament. Nearly everyone who
asked Jesus to intervene in their lives or meet a need first came
and bowed down before Him *first*. Worship involves bowing our
hearts (and bodies at times) before God. God is looking for a people who will prostrate themselves in their heart and lavishly give
themselves to praise. They will create an atmosphere for a throne
of praise in which God Himself is pleased to dwell! When we
prostrate ourselves and lavishly give our hearts in praise and in
adoration to Him, we are creating a place in the spirit from which
He will rule and reign over His enemies.

> **Nearly everyone who asked Jesus to
> intervene in their lives or meet a need first
> came and bowed down before Him *first*.**

The Syro-Phenocian woman in Matthew 15:25 prostrated herself before Jesus first. Then she asked Him for a miracle. Prayer
and worship are mentioned as interactive integral parts of the first
church. Acts 16:25 describes how Paul and Silas, their backs
stinging and bleeding, boldly prayed and worshiped God aloud—
even while bound in stocks.

It was also impossible to separate praise and prayer in the Old
Testament. Jewish worshipers often sang God's praise and slipped

smoothly into prayer and back again. The two were uniquely interjoined and were never intended to be separated. The Lord declared, "Even those I will bring to My holy mountain, and make them joyful in My house of prayer" (Is. 56:7a). The Hebrew word for prayer here is *tephillah*. It is used to describe prayer 77 times in the Old Testament, and it refers to "intercession, supplication; by implication *a hymn*—prayer."[2] Another source implies several meanings including intercession, to the act of intervening, judgment, and broken supplication.[3]

My condensed definition of this kind of prayer is based on David, psalmist's decision to label his psalm-hymns as prayers. I call the *tephillah* the "*the sung intercessory judgments of God.*" This term specifically is used to title the five greatest psalms of David—Psalms 17; 86; 90; 102; and 142. It also is used in the title for the prayer of Habbakkuk in Habbakkuk 3:1. This was a joining together of the high priestly ministry of prayer and of praise.

In Psalm 72:20, the Bible says, "The *prayers* of David the son of Jesse are ended." Again, David the psalmist uses the plural of the word here, *tephillah*, meaning "the sung intercessory judgments of God." This reference to Psalms 1 through 72 clearly tells us that they were all "sung prayers." They were most likely set to music and sung in formal worship.

A Divine Appointment

Now that we better understand what the Lord means when He says His house is to be a "house of prayer for all nations," we need to go back to the number "37." After our encounter with the Lord in the watch tower at Herrnhut in 1993, Michal Ann and I took the team of intercessors to the city of Liebreac in the Czech Republic. Three years earlier in 1990, I had visited Prague with my dear brother, Mahesh Chavda about six months after communism fell. He conducted a massive gathering where 10,000 people came, and we prayed for people for healing until 2:00 in the morning every night. One year later, I was invited to speak at their national conference in Prague, and upon its completion took my team to northern Czech to this quaint city called Libreac. One day, when the other people in our ministry team took a day off and went out touring, I stayed in my room to seek the Lord. Only one thing came to me that day. God wanted me to meet a man who had received a heavenly vision.

I was scheduled to speak at a church in the city that night, and I'd never met the leadership of the church. I didn't even know what kind of church it was. I noticed that the senior pastor wasn't on the platform, but I didn't realize that he was sitting in the congregation to the side of the platform that night. I stood up to speak, and about halfway through, the Lord had me point to this person on the side and say: "Sir, you've had a heavenly visitation. You have been taken up in the Spirit before God, and He spoke to you about ten things that are going to happen. And you are going to be used to help restore the Watch of the Lord."

I did not know that this man, Pastor Evald Ruffy, was a Moravian pastor of this congregation of 13 people which since has grown to a vibrant church of a few hundred. During communism, it had been a little group. Earlier in the year, Evald had traveled to Sweden. While he was preaching, he had a heart attack and went into a coma for a few days. His associate pastor, Peter, was also his best friend. Evald told me later that he "went on a little trip for three days" and saw the Lord. He looked down upon the globe much like Ezekiel was "hung between heaven and earth" (Ezek. 8:3). Evald saw dark clouds over central Europe penetrated by white lights going up and down from the heavens. The Holy Spirit explained, "These are My angels being released in answer to the prayers of the saints." They were breaking up the black clouds which were territorial spirits massed over central Europe.

On the third day of Evald's heavenly visit, his best friend, Peter, joined Evald's wife at the bedside of his dear friend whom he believed was sinking into an irreversible coma. Peter didn't know how to pray for his friend. Evald, whose spirit seemed to be in Heaven at the time, did not realize that he was a husband, a father, and a pastor whose work was incomplete. He was just enjoying Heaven. Then Peter began to pray a "prayer of tears" from his heart. As Peter's tears fell from his eyes and landed on Evald's body in the hospital bed, Evald suddenly began to be aware in Heaven that he was a husband, a father, and a pastor, and that his work was not yet complete. He also knew that he had a decision to make.

> **Evald [Ruffy] saw dark clouds over central Europe penetrated by white lights going up and down from the heavens. The Holy Spirit explained, "These are My angels being released in answer to the prayers of the saints."**

Within moments, Evald found himself soaring through the heavens. Then his spirit hit his body in the hospital bed. He was miraculously healed in a moment. The doctors declared it a miracle. He was released from the hospital and didn't have to pay a dime of the medical expenses! Today, I know the story well. But that night in 1991, I just said, "There's a man over here whose had a heavenly visitation." Evald responded, and the rest is history. The people in that service passed around a sign-up list. People signed up that very night to launch a renewed Watch of the Lord—and they haven't stopped. They have one of the most vital churches in all of the Czech Republic today, and recently started eight satellite churches. I believe Evald is operating in an authentic apostolic call today.

Kneeling in the Streets!

So in 1993, fresh from our Herrnhut encounter, we found ourselves back in Evald's city of Libreac. We divided our prayer group into smaller teams to stay in the homes of the people there, and my wife and I led a small group to an area called Heineson where a satellite church was being planted. Michal Ann and I were walking down a little cobblestone street in the company of some of church leaders and members when I noticed some little white objects scattered on the street.

I looked closer at these objects and felt faith start to rise up in me. I pointed them out to Michal Ann, who began to get excited, too. The objects looked like white marbles. For some reason I felt like we were supposed to pick them up. (I love the Holy Ghost. He is not only good, but He is also lots of fun.) So Michal Ann and I got down on our hands and knees to pick up these marbles on a cobblestone street in the Czech Republic while it drizzled rain upon us. I think the local church leaders who were watching us were wondering if we'd lost our marbles! The truth is that "we found them that day." These marbles looked like they were hand-made from white stone of some kind. After we picked up every single marble, we felt led to count them while the leaders waited for us. Guess how many we found? Thirty-seven!

Little keys open big doors. The symbolic interpretation of this little incident came instantly: "The Church 'lost her marbles' some time ago, and we have lost the mind of Christ about the heavenly perspective of the eternal value of prayer!" God has something on His mind—Ezekiel 37. God is out to return His marbles, the mind of Christ, to His Church, because she's lost her way. We are regaining His eternal perspective on the value of the prayers of two or three who come together in the name of Jesus! He wants to give us back the key of power released when believers harmonize together in the name of Jesus. In your life and ministry, understanding may only require one simple and humble step: Ask. My wife and I couldn't figure out why we were so excited that day in Heineson, and those local church leaders couldn't either—until we started counting our marbles. (I still have these precious 37 marbles to this day on display on our fireplace mantle.)

Prayer Precedes Missions

Organized missionary work and world evangelization as we know it today really didn't exist in the Western world until God lit a fire in the hearts of the Moravians through the watch of the Lord. It was no accident that God restored the fire on the altar of prayer *first*, and then He ignited a passion for lost souls in and through prayer. Let me quote from Leslie K. Tarr's account once more:

"Six months after the beginning of the prayer watch, the count [von Zinzendorf] suggested to his fellow Moravians the challenge of a bold evangelism aimed at the West Indies, Greenland, Turkey, and Lapland. Some were skeptical, but Zinzendorf persisted. Twenty-six Moravians stepped forward for world missions wherever the Lord led."[4]

By 1832, 100 years after the first missionaries left for foreign soil, 42 Moravian mission stations existed around the world. Today, membership in the Moravian mission churches outnumber those at home 4-to-1.[5]

> **It was no accident that God restored the fire on the altar of prayer *first*, and then He ignited a passion for lost souls in and through prayer.**

Today, every 60 minutes about 7,000 people die of which 6,000, do not know the Lord Jesus Christ. There are 235 geographical entities called nations of which 97 have been virtually closed to conventional residential missionary activity. An estimated 2.6 billion unreached people live in these closed nations in what has been called "The 10/40 Window." Millions of Christians recently have banded together to pray and intercede for these people, but this one-time or two-time effort is only the beginning of what God is doing in His Church.[6]

We can see a picture of God's goal in Revelation 5:8-10. Jesus taught us to pray, "Thy will be done, on earth as it is in heaven" (Mt. 6:10). According to this passage in the Book of Revelation, the redeemed of God in Heaven come from every tribe, every tongue and people and nation. They were involved in unceasing worship and praise of the Lord!

Heaven on Earth

I'll never forget the wonderful sound of worship in a service held in Williamstadt, the capital of the island nation of Curaso, one of the Netherlands Antilles islands just off the coast of Venezuela where approximately 136,000 people live. What struck me was how these people worshiped! Their worship service was conducted in four languages at once! They sang in Dutch, English, Spanish, and in their own island dialect called Palpamento. It was wonderful. It was a taste of Heaven. At one moment they would sing the praises of Jesus in English; then they would sing in Dutch. They would sing "I Exalt Thee" in Spanish, then in Papamento, and finally in English. They displayed multiple expressions in dance and in prayer. I thought, *Lord, I like this.* I felt as if He replied, "If you like this, wait till you get up here with Me!"

Jesus Christ is transforming us into a "house of prayer." He longs for us to lavishly pour our fears, our love, our affection, our adoration, and our tears upon the feet of Jesus. He longs to hear us say again and again, "God, I lay my life before You." As we do this, He will shine His face upon us in all of His glory and say, "Go. Your feet are shod with the preparation of the gospel of peace."

In Psalm 2:8, God says, "Ask of Me, and I will surely give the nations as Thine inheritance, and the very ends of the earth as Thy possession." A lot of voices in the church world will say, "You can have the world—I don't want it. This country is going to hell—but I'm going to Heaven." Sometimes, we are too ready to give away the very thing God wants to give to us just because there are some giants in the land. God still needs some Joshuas and Calebs today.

He is looking for a people who will stand in the gap and say, "Yes, Lord, I am looking for the rewards of Christ's suffering. I'm asking for the nations as a footstool for Your marvelous feet." God wants to see a whole nation of kings and priests offer this prayer to him with faith, power, and passion.

Keys to the Harvest

No harvest can take place without prayer for four very important reasons:

1. Only a small part of God's people who are involved in seed sowing.
2. Only a small part of the seed sown actually germinates.

3. Only a small part of the seed that germinates continues growing to full harvest.
4. Only a small part of the actual harvest is fully utilized.

Your prayers can make a vital difference, especially when you harmonize in prayer with others and carefully target your prayers. Since prayer is unhindered by time, distance, or language barriers, you can join any ministry team on the earth! Teams can go constantly to sow the seed of the gospel in the earth. For God's sake, get on somebody's team. Pray for ministry leaders and help them see something make it to harvest! Remember, through prayer you can join any team! You are not confined by time, distance, or space. Ask God to guide you to the ministry or persons He wants you to support in prayer. He will burden your heart. You will become a modern-day Aaron or Hur lifting up the weary hands of your God-appointed Moses.

Your prayers can "water" the harvest and energize the seed that has been sown. Perhaps the greatest need between seed time and harvest is rain. Spiritually speaking, enough seed has been sown to bring millions to Christ! There is no fault in the seed. The problem is water. The extent of the harvest can depend upon the amount of prayer that waters the seed.

> **Join with Ezra, Nehemiah, Esther, Deborah, and Daniel—whose prayers changed the heart of rulers, altered the laws of the land, and influenced national leaders.**

Your prayers can help cultivate the crop. Jesus warned that the trouble, persecution, worries of this life, and deceitfulness of wealth would cause some to drop by the wayside and become unfruitful (Mt. 13:20-22). Your prayers can encourage, strengthen, and protect the germinated seed during the critical period when new life comes up.

Your prayer actually can influence world leaders and activate the resources of God! Proverbs 21:1 says, "The king's heart is like channels of water in the hand of the Lord; He turns it like a wherever He wishes." Join with Ezra, Nehemiah, ___, Deborah, and Daniel—whose prayers changed the heart of rulers, altered the laws of the land, and influenced national leaders.

Praying for the Harvest

I have a friend named Dick Simmons who is one of the overlooked key intercessory people in this nation. More than 30 years ago, Dick was attending Bible college in New York City. He was marked for intercession. In the middle of the night on the bank of the Hudson River, he began to cry out to the Lord in intercession for New York City. He prayed at the top of his lungs, "Lord, I beseech Thee that You send forth laborers unto Your field!" His agonized prayers were so loud at 2:00 a.m. (even by New York City standards!) that he suddenly was bathed in floodlights on the riverbank. Cautious police officers shouted out, "What are you doing? You have been reported for disturbing the peace because you've been waking up people!"

Dick bellowed back, "Oh, I am just praying to the Lord of the harvest that He would send forth laborers into His field."

The police officers must have been shocked, or else they agreed with Brother Simmons. They let him go without any charges or warning. That very night, the Holy Spirit of God descended on a little skinny preacher in rural Pennsylvania and gave him a divine call to take the gospel to New York City. Do you know his name? It was David Wilkerson. It is no wonder that when David Wilkerson established the first Teen Challenge Center in New York City, he chose Dick Simmons to be its first director.

I tell you the truth: If you dare to echo the prayers of Jesus, your petition will pierce the heavens and the Father, Himself, will receive it. Then, as the bowls of prayer are tipped over, He will send it hurtling back at the speed of light to the earth to effect His divine will and judgment on the matter! Study God's Word and learn how to pray with power and effectiveness. Begin to pray the tenfold claim of the Colossians in Colossians 1:9-12:

For this reason also, since the day we heard of it, we have not ceased to pray for you and to ask that you may be filled with the knowledge of His will in all spiritual wisdom and understanding, so that you may walk in a manner worthy of the Lord, to please Him in all respects, bearing fruit in every good work and increasing in the knowledge of God; strengthened with all power, according to His glorious might, for the attaining of all steadfastness and patience; joyously giving thanks to the Father, who has qualified us to share in the inheritance of the saints in light (Colossians 1:9-12).

Wisdom Applications

Dick Eastman lists five claims of revelation and five claims of blessing on this passage in his book, *Love on Its Knees*, which I've adapted for this chapter:[7]

Five Claims of Revelation

1. Pray for a revelation of *God's will* for the gospel worker, a person, or people. This prayer is for divine direction.
2. Pray for a revelation of *God's wisdom*, or divine perception. This is a prayer that the person would not only be filled with the knowledge of God's will, but that he or she would also know *how to implement it* in a wise manner.
3. Pray for a revelation of *God's understanding* or comprehension. This means that the person will know what the Father has for him or her to do, how to do it—as well as when, where, and with whom.
4. Pray for a revelation of *God's holiness* so the person will walk worthy of the Lord and please Him in every way.
5. Pray for a revelation of *God's pleasure* or divine gratification. This is really key. You need to pray for this for your own life and for the lives of those whom God has laid on your heart. Pray that they would have a revelation of the pleasure God finds in them and their work of obedience. Also pray for Jesus to become their chief pleasure. In reality, this is a prayer for intimacy.

Five Claims of Blessing

1. Pray for *increased effectiveness*, productivity, and fruitfulness. Pray that the persons will become more fruitful in every good work and deed.
2. Pray for their *increased devotional growth* or spirituality. Pray that they might know Him and draw near to Him in increased intimacy.
3. Pray for an *increase of strength.* You could call this "increased durability," where the worker or person will have a thick skin like a rhinoceros, but with a tender heart.
4. Pray for an *increase of patience.*
5. Pray for an *increase of joy.* Pray that they will have an increased delight in the work of the Lord. Ask God to bless them and pray for a bucket of joy to be dumped on their heads. The joy of the Lord is our strength (Neh. 8:10).

How Will the Harvest Come?

The great harvest of the Lord never will be accomplished by a few hired hands, nor even by a team of highly gifted evangelists, apostles, prophets, teachers, and pastors. The work is too great, the scope too grand to be accomplished by an elite few—only a praying church can harvest an entire lost world in one generation! God is calling every member of His household back to the foundation of prayer that launches every great move of God in the earth. It is time for us to hit our knees and pray the heart of God into being in the earth! It's time for us to recapture our marbles and have the mind of Christ concerning the "House of Prayer for All Nations."

Endnotes

1. Strong's, **worship** (#4352).

2. Strong's, **prayer** (#8605).

3. *Theological Wordbook of the Old Testament, Vol. 2,* **prayer** (*lepilla*, Hebrew #1776a), 725-726, provides the descriptive words noted in my text, although I have not quoted directly from this reference work.

4. Tarr, "A Prayer Meeting."

5. "The World of 1732," *Christian History* Magazine (Worchester, Pennsylvania, 1982) Vol. I, No. 1, 13.

6. Dick Eastman, *Love on Its Knees* (Grand Rapids: Chosen Books, 1989), 105. Selected statistics and data were drawn from this excellent book on prayer and the harvest.

7. Eastman, *Love.*

Chapter 8

Restoring the Expectation of the Supernatural

The old priest's hands trembled as they slowly dropped finely ground bits of freshly mixed incense on the ancient altar of incense in Herod's temple. "How many times have I entered this place and done this very same thing before the Presence?" old Zachariah asked himself. The haunting sound of the unceasing chants, moans, and cries of the people praying outside the Holy Place could still be heard, even though several feet of solid stone walls and the thick veil of separation had dulled their force in part.

Reciting ancient intercessory prayers from the Torah dating back to Moshe (Moses), Zachariah the priest felt a strange thrill rush through his body as a thought long forgotten rose unbidden to his mind: *Why don't you ask for yourself?* Taking the last pinch of incense in his right hand, he gently dropped it into the flickering flames of the smoking fire on the altar and whispered to the Presence he could almost feel through the thick veil:

"O Holy God of Abraham, Isaac, and Jacob, from birth I have been called Zachariah, 'Yah has remembered,' and my lovely Elisabeth has been called 'God of the Oath'; yet the name we hear the most is 'barren.' Would you remember me, Ancient One, though I have no heir? You have declared You would bless those who seek You, and I seek you this day. Grant me my heart's desire that we may praise and worship You in the company of a son before we die. Then our very names will declare the truth and mercy in Thy name, Holy One."[1]

Suddenly, the dim flickering light from the 12 flames of the golden candlestick in the Holy Place were eclipsed by a blinding light and a paralyzing sense of awe. As Zechariah suddenly spun around to see where the light came from, he had a sinking feeling in the pit of his stomach. "I'm a dead man!" he thought. "I've transgressed against the Amighty and am undone... "The moment his eyes stopped on the brilliant figure standing to the side of the altar of incense, he was nearly overcome with terror and fear.

But the angel said to him, "Do not be afraid, Zacharias, for your petition has been heard, and your wife Elizabeth will bear you a son, and you will give him the name John. And you will have joy and gladness, and many will rejoice at his birth" (Luke 1:13b-14).

Moments later, old Zachariah staggered out of the Holy Place trembling and rubbing his eyes with tears soaking his priestly robes. The other priests rushed to him and peppered him with urgent questions about what had happened and why he had been gone so long. They soon realized the priest they had known most of their lives was a changed man. God must have visited him in the Holy Place, because he could no longer speak. Some thought Zachariah had been cursed for a transgression of some kind and figured he was lucky just to be alive, but others who knew him well thought differently.

In time, they would all know exactly what had happened in the Holy Place that day. The truth is that in that intimate scheme of the old, represented by the trappings of priestly worship with bloody sacrifice, fire, and temporary atonement, God had birthed the new. Gabriel, the archangel of God, met Zachariah in the Holy Place and announced God's answer to his fervent prayer, but the priest's unbelief caused him to lose his ability to talk. It was Elisabeth, whose name literally means "the oath of God," who would carry God's promised son in her aged womb for nine months from the time Zachariah returned home. She mysteriously disappeared from public view for the first five months, and many of the gossipers in the city swore she was trying to escape the public ridicule that had met her everyday at the markets and even during the temple gatherings on holy days.

Zachariah would not and could not speak for nine long months after his supernatural encounter. But on the eighth day after the miraculous birth of his son, John, the first words the aged priest uttered as he gazed on the new life destined to prepare the way for eternal life were words of worship and praise to God (Lk. 1:64). Zachariah's supernatural encounter with Gabriel is a wonderful picture of the way God intervenes in the affairs of men.

> **Those of us who are filled with *His* desire and *His* secrets find ourselves launched on a journey of supernatural encounters, intercession, and intervention as we speak forth the decrees of God in the earth by His Spirit!**

Zachariah began the process with a dedicated, consecrated life that was blameless in God's sight. He stood in the office of priest offering sacrifices of prayer and praise to God on behalf of others, to the accompaniment of corporate prayer and intercession. He finally asked God to act on his behalf, and the fruit of his prayer became a blessing to all the world and every generation afterward. He didn't realize that his secret heart's desire had been God's desire all along. His petition—bathed in worship and praise and carried to the heart of God in personal and corporate prayer— caused the ancient seed of God, His Word and promises, to be planted in the earth as a new seed of supernatural intervention to be revealed in the fulness of time.

The Kiss of God on Our Hearts

God longs to see us linger before Him and offer the incense of prayer and praise on the fire of our passion for Him. If we do, we will soon find their hearts filled with the very desires and secrets of God. Those of us who are filled with *His* desire and *His* secrets find ourselves launched on a journey of supernatural encounters, intercession, and intervention as we speak forth the decrees of God in the earth by His Spirit! We can literally blend the power of the unchanging Ancient of days with the faith He gives us today to create something new and holy in the earth. What a privilege we have in our ability to pray in Jesus' name!

Then IT Happened!

The wind was blowing fiercely outside our house just before midnight on October 6, 1992. It was the Day of Atonement, the ancient day of sacrifice, salvation, and new beginnings observed by Jews around the world for thousands of years. At 11:59 p.m., I was suddenly awakened by a crash of lightning that brightly illuminated our bedroom. In the eerie flickering light in our backyard I saw a man standing in our room. He looked straight at me...

I blinked and looked at him again, and he continued to look at me for what seemed like the longest minute of my life. Then I heard the words, "Watch your wife. I'm about to speak to her." Michal Ann was still asleep when the being spoke to me, but when the clock reached the midnight hour, the manifested *appearance* seemed to leave the room. I could sense the being's presence although I could no longer see him. Michal Ann instantly woke up, and trembling in the fear of the Lord, I whispered to her, "An angel has just come!" Together we shook in the bed with the covers pulled up right to our faces for the next 30 minutes. Tyler, our four-year-old son, had moved to our room when he had become frightened by the storm, and he was asleep on the floor on my side of the bed through the whole ordeal. For some reason, I floated off to sleep for a while without telling Michal Ann what the "man" had said. She was now left wide awake as the sense of the presence increased and I slumbered away.

While I slept, the Holy Spirit began to move upon Michal Ann in some rather unusual ways. At one point she felt a hand in the middle of her back exerting great pressure, and she heard herself moaning and groaning as the activity increased. It was so intense that she was afraid to even look at herself in the mirror, thinking she might discover that her hair had turned white or the appearance of her face had been dramatically rearranged. Just as this portion of the intense encounter came to an end, I woke up again. A light was shining over our bedroom dresser. We continued to tremble as the fear of the Lord was ever so strong. We tossed up a feeble prayer and said, "Lord if this visitation is of You, then cause for one of our children to have a dream about an angel to confirm this visitation." We waited and quietly prayed, "Oh God, oh God, oh God!" I think we identified with the old gospel hymn, "Were You There?" in the line where it says, "Sometimes He causes me to tremble, tremble, tremble." I then fell asleep for the rest of the night, but Michal Ann was left alone again until 5:00 a.m. with God's terrifying Presence thick in the room.

Later that morning we awakened to find Tyler standing right beside me, and He said, "I had a dream last night that an angel come and visited our house." Justin, our first born, was asleep in his room right above us on the second floor. He was all excited that morning when he told us that he, too, had a dream that angels had come. In the dream he was shown a white horse that was being prepared for a mission that was yet to come. Interesting, huh? Michal Ann was shown the same horse when at one point she seemed to have been "taken up in the Spirit." How comforting and reassuring this was! God was watching over His word to perform it. Remember, when something is truly of the Lord, He will confirm it by the witness of two and three.

A Dream Beforehand

Although we were somewhat already versed in the supernatural activities of the Holy Spirit, this was a totally new league. But it's interesting to note, that in the summer of 1992, I had a dream in which the Lord instructed me to study the ministry and function of angels. I avidly read all the Scriptures on the subject and every book that I could find. I thought it was an interesting assignment, but I had no idea that in the fall of that year our household would become a "visitation ground" for angels. Nor would I have guessed that for the following nine weeks the visitations would center primarily around my wife. At this point, you'll have to hear the rest of the story from Michal Ann herself:

"I heard a spiritual song in my sleep that I just couldn't figure out. It bothered me so much that I woke up. The singer in this dream sang, 'Where is my bride, oh my God?' I pondered those words over and over until I finally realized that it was Jesus who was singing the song.

"I was getting some clarity on some of the issues brought up by the Holy Spirit at that point, but it was very overwhelming. I didn't know what to do with the song, and this really bothered me because I felt that it had much to do with Jesus' return to claim His spotless Bride, the Church.

"The problem is that as a Bride we don't know what we should look like, and we don't really know what our Groom looks like either. He is coming, *and we don't intimately know who He is!* I felt a deep burden to search out His face and to *know Him* just for His sake. As if in answer to my quest, the Lord sent angelic visitors into our bedroom night after night for the next nine weeks, and each time they came, they ushered in the manifest Presence of God. This weighty glory of God was almost unbearable to me. I was scared out of my wits because the fear of the Lord was so intense.

"One time I saw 12 fireballs literally arch through the room and hit me squarely in the chest. Their impact electrified my body and made me wonder if I was going to survive the experience. Before the arrival of the Presence each night, I would earnestly pray to experience God's fulness again. As His glory filled my bedroom, I would feel the pressing weight of His holiness and begin to cry out, 'Please Lord, I can't take anymore! I think I am going to die!' "

"Finally, the Lord said, "'Ann, do you want Me to come or not?' I took several days to think over this question because I was just so overwhelmed by the intensity of His Presence.

**"I felt a deep burden to search out His face and to *know Him* just for His sake. As if in answer to my quest, the Lord sent angelic visitors into our bedroom night after night for the next nine weeks, and each time they came, they would usher in the manifest Presence of God. This weighty glory of God was almost unbearable to me."
—Michal Ann Goll**

"In His mercy, the Lord brought me to a place where I had to decide what really mattered the most to me. He was no longer willing to let me just waffle back and forth from day to day and retreat into my excuses and fears. Perhaps it was a form of the 'Mount Moriah' test and God wanted to see if I was willing to climb upon the altar of God myself as a living sacrifice. Finally, the Lord confronted me with a choice—not a choice between salvation or damnation, for I was already forgiven and saved since a child—but a choice to make between what I had already experienced and what God longed yet to impart to me. The problem was that He wanted me to empty my hands before He filled them with something greater. He asked me, 'Well, what do you want?'

"Finally, I responded to Him in the way He always wanted me to respond. I said, 'Well Lord, if I live, I live; and if I die, I die. But I really, really want You to come.' Angelic visitors continued to visit our bedroom regularly. They still visit on occasion. In every case, they always speak of the things that are nearest and dearest to the heart of God. At times we are struck with ecstasy, and at other times we become struck low with the fear of God and a stark revelation of our sinfulness compared to His incomparable holiness and beauty.

"I came out of these times of visitation with a burden to help men and women get ready for His coming—His intimate, personal coming. Every time that I hear some of the songs we sing with incredible words and melodies about intimacy with God, I tremble. When we sing, 'Oh Lord, let me feel the kisses of Your mouth, let me feel Your warm embrace, feel the tenderness of Your touch...' and the like, I'm convinced experiencially that *we have no idea what His kiss is like*!

"Just as I pulled back when the manifest Presence of God entered my room with unexpected results, we as a corporate body of believers often recoil when He really answers our sung prayers and touches us with His glory and fire! We back up and say, 'No! You're coming too close.' Meanwhile, God is saying, 'Do you realize that all of those songs you've been singing to Me are arousing My love? I am coming to you and you don't even know that it's Me.' "

Changed by His Presence

After the most intense period of these angelic visitations had passed, I walked into our kitchen one night, looked at Michal Ann, and said, "I just don't know who you are anymore." She looked at me and replied, *"I just don't know who I am becoming."* Since then, I've seen a new depth of raw power and spiritual authority rise up in Michal Ann's life. God imparted something to her that allows her to see past the barriers of fear, and she is able to minister security, hope, and destiny with authority. Even people who have never known Michal Ann before recognize that someone or something incredible has totally transformed her into a mighty woman and minister of God. This highlights one of the most dynamic roles of supernatural encounters in our lives.

Presence Evangelism

What does this subject of "Restoring the Expectation of the Supernatural" have to do with the lost art of intercession and the great harvest? Everything! Once again, I want to share a supernatural experience my wife had in which the Lord demonstrated to her *one of His ways* of winning the lost to Christ. She told me about a series of dreams that she had concerning the Lord's desire to touch the Jewish people. She saw herself standing beside me. We were facing three very tall Jewish men with black beards and heavy hair. Their arms were folded, and they were looking sternly at Michal Ann as if to say in judgment, "Who do you think you are that God would use *you* to bring the gospel to the Jews?"

Michal Ann remembers looking at these men and saying, "You are absolutely right. I am nobody. There isn't a reason in the world why God should choose me. It is only by the anointing of the Lord that we can do anything." Then she began to turn the conversation from the men and toward the Lord. Then she began to cry out to the Lord with words the Lord gave her to say: "Release Your anointing, Lord! Release Your Presence and Your Spirit so that revelation will come and the blinders will fall off of their eyes."

In this dream, a spotlight suddenly shone from Heaven upon Michal Ann. Immediately the three critical men were all struck by the light. Instantly, they lifted their hands to their mouths and took a step back. Then they began to declare, "I see!" The favor of the Lord had been released and a major turning point had been reached. Where the Jewish men had been closed to the gospel before they saw the light, now they were suddenly open to receive the truth about the Messiah.

Michal Ann told me that she felt like she is walking down a path of discovery—not just with ministry to the Jewish people, but in the whole ministry field:

"It's almost like that is my life story. I feel like God looked down from Heaven and picked the most unlikely, insecure, fearful person for the job.

"It doesn't depend on the person, It depends on God and His infilling power. That's the only way that I can do anything, go anywhere, or have any anointing. When Jim and I first began to travel together, he would speak and then he would call people up for ministry. I dreaded it because he would always turn to me and say: 'Okay Ann, you start over on that side and I'll start over here.'

"In my case, God shined His light on me said, 'I choose *you*!' He didn't ask for my opinion or the opinion of anyone else on the matter. "
—Michal Ann Goll

"I used to feel like a duck out of water. I didn't know what to do. I felt so awkward that I just wanted to evaporate down into a little puddle and go underneath the door so nobody would notice that I had slipped out. I would try to pray, and I'd watch Jim to see what he was doing, but it just fell flat. You know what? God wasn't upset by that at all. He wasn't upset at making me uncomfortable or putting me the spotlight on me. He allowed me time to become secure in Him. This should bring hope to every person, regardless of gender, race, or age. It doesn't depend on us—it depends on the Lord alone. When you adjust the way you operate to accommodate this truth, then you can do things, and God can use you in any way that He sees fit. All you have to do is make yourself available. In my case, God shined His light on me said, 'I choose *you*!'

He didn't ask for my opinion or the opinion of anyone else on the matter."

I watched the Lord impart to Michal Ann a supernatural grace, favor, and anointing to do His bidding. In fact, He has come to both of us in ways that we wouldn't even know how to ask for.

The Purpose of the Supernatural

Why do we need to restore the "expectation of supernatural encounters"? One reason is found in Ephesians 6:12 which says, "For our struggle is not against flesh and blood, but against the rulers, against the powers, against the world forces of this darkness, against the spiritual forces of wickedness in the heavenly places." When you face a supernatural adversary, you *must* defeat him by supernatural means. The illusory weapons of the flesh and physical realm mean nothing to spirit beings—whether they are holy or unholy.

The second reason is that in every true revival in human history, evidence of signs and wonders confirm the Word that was preached. These "signs following" were a beacon to the unsaved declaring that God is alive and well. He is still in the soul-saving, miracle-working business. "And they went forth, and preached every where, the Lord working with them, and confirming the word with signs following. Amen" (Mk. 16:20 KJV).

The third reason has to do with the nature of God who is Spirit, and the ordained purpose of God's most powerful and mysterious servants, the angels. By definition, it is impossible for our supernatural God who is Spirit to step into our death-bound, flesh-dominated world apart from supernatural means. That is why liberal theologians around the world work so hard to disprove and cast aside every reference to the supernatural in the Bible—they fear the idea that God is truly God and that He intervenes supernaturally in the affairs of men and women. Such a God is totally uncontrollable and even unpredictable! This is totally unacceptable to professional religious scholars who have never personally encountered the supernatural God.

116   The Lost Art of Intercession

Let me briefly outline the three primary functions and at least 15 activities of angels involved in the affairs of God and man:

Three Primary Functions of Angels

1. They continually offer praise and worship to God.

Praise Him, all His angels; Praise Him, all His hosts! (Psalm 148:2).

Let them praise the name of the Lord, For He commanded and they were created (Psalm. 148:5).

2. They are sent as "flames of fire" and "winds of God" to minister to mankind.

And of the angels He says, "Who makes his angels winds, and His ministers a flame of fire" (Hebrews 1:7).

Are they not all ministering spirits, sent out to render service for the sake of those who will inherit salvation? (Hebrews 1:14).

3. Angels were created to excel in strength and obey the voice of His word so they could perform God's Word.

Bless the Lord, you His angels, mighty in strength, who perform His word, obeying the voice of his word! bless the Lord, all you His hosts, you who serve Him, doing His will (Psalm 103:20-21).

Types of Angelic Activities

1. They minister the Presence of the Lord (Is. 63:9; Rev. 18:1).
2. They are messengers sent to pronounce God's will (Mt. 1:20; 2:13,19; 28:1-7; Lk. 1:19,26).
3. They release understanding in dreams and visions (Dan. 8:15-19; 9:23; Rev. 1:1).
4. They help give guidance and direction (Acts 8:26; 27:23-24,29; Gen. 24:7,40).
5. They bring deliverance (2 Kings 19:35; Is. 37:36).
6. They provide protection (Ps. 34:7; 91:11-12; Mt. 18:10).

7. They are present upon the death of the saints (Ps. 23:4; 116:15; Lk. 16:22; Jude 9).
8. They release strength (Dan. 10:16-18; Mt. 4:11; Lk. 22:43).
9. They are used as healing instruments in the hands of God (Jn. 5:4).
10. They continually offer praise and worship to God (Gen. 32:1-2; Lk. 2:14; Rev. 5:11-12).
11. They bind demonic powers at God's bidding (Dan. 10:13; Rev. 12:7; 20:1-3).
12. They serve as divine watchers (Dan. 4:13,17; Acts 12:20-23; 1 Tim. 5:21).
13. They help reap many of the harvests of God (Mt. 13:39-42; 24:31; Rev. 14:6, 14-19).
14. They execute the judgments of God (Gen. 19:11; Ex. 12:18-30, 2 Kings 19:35; Acts 12:20-23; Rev. 16:17).

Our interactions with angels hinge on five basic premises:
1. **We are co-workers with Christ,** and as such, God's resources are released by man's invitation in accordance with His will. Intercession releases angelic intervention.
2. **Answered prayers influence or help to determine the destiny of individuals and nations.**
3. **There is an innumerable company of angels waiting to be dispatched** (unemployed angels, if you will). "As the host of heaven cannot be counted, and the sand of the sea cannot be measured" (Jer. 33:22a).
4. **Angels are involved in virtually all of the everyday, practical affairs of men.** They are involved in virtually every facet of everyday life and the normal activities of mankind.
5. **Angels are often utilized by God to deliver or execute His answers to our prayers.**

Angelic Intervention Through Intercession

Many examples of angelic intervention stand out in the Bible. Abraham interceded for Sodom and Gomorrah and held back

118   *The Lost Art of Intercession*

judgment until Lot's family could be saved by angelic couriers (Gen. 19:1-29). Daniel persisted in intercession until the angel Gabriel, himself, arrived after battling the dark prince of Persia on behalf of Daniel and the Jewish people (Dan. 10:12-21). The New Testament record also tells us about three different instances where prayer and the supernatural intervention of angels led to the deliverance of early Church disciples from prison. Peter, the apostle, was personally escorted out of an impregnable prison by an angel dispatched in response the to the single-hearted prayers of the saints in Jerusalem in Acts 12:7-10).

So Peter was kept in the prison, but prayer for him was being made fervently by the church to God. And on the very night when Herod was about to bring him forward, Peter was sleeping between two soldiers, bound with two chains; and guards in front of the door were watching over the prison. And behold, an angel of the Lord suddenly appeared, and a light shone in the cell; and he struck Peter's side and roused him, saying, "Get up quickly." And the chains fell off his hands (Acts 12:5-7).

In this instance, it was *prayer* that delivered Paul from Herod's murderous schemes (Acts 12:5). The fervent unified prayers of the 120 believers waiting for the coming of the Holy Spirit nearly a year earlier had caused the place to be swept with wind and fire in Acts 2:2-6. Then beginning in Acts 16:26, the sacrificial praise and worship of Paul and Silas offered from their stocks in the prison at Jerusalem triggered a violent earthquake and angelic deliverance for them!

I've already described the vision recieved by Evald Ruffy, the Moravian pastor from the Czech Republic, who saw angels going back and forth between Heaven and earth in response to the prayer of the saints. We've also examined my family's experiences with angelic visitors in the night. You probably think these stories are pretty exciting, but you may automatically exempt yourself from such "special experiences." Don't.

We are about to move into another phase in the powerful move of God on the earth. We've experienced a "second Pentecost," if you will, characterized by the new wine of joy and refreshing that swept through churches across the world. Then the Lord stepped up the pace and ignited the fires of repentance, cleansing, and holiness when He suddenly descended on the Father's Day service at Brownsville Assembly of God in Pensacola, Florida. Now we are entering into a third level characterized by *power*.

I Will Restore Pentecost

In this third wave, the Holy Spirit will be utilizing the gift of workings of miracles throughout the Body of Christ. The Lord told me before all of this began, "I will restore Pentecost." The advent of the Holy Spirit on Pentecost was marked by three signs: the wind of the Spirit's coming; the fire of the holiness and purity of God indwelling believers; and the intoxicating effect of the wine of the Spirit on mankind.

> **We've feasted on the wine of the Spirit and have been refreshed with laughter, joy, and renewal. We have bowed our knees in humility and repentance under the fiery presence of our jealous God, the righteous King of glory. We have been lifted up in His grace as righteous, holy, and pure in His sight. Now, we are about to experience the *wind of God*, characterized by powerful supernatural gifts, supernatural encounters, and angelic intervention!**

The first phase of God's appearing fell on Toronto in 1994. Paul Cain described it by saying, "God was serving the appetizer." The Spirit of God fell on Pensacola in 1995 with holy fire that restored the fear of the Lord (and the corresponding understanding of His immeasurable grace) to the Church. Now, we are about to go deeper. In September of 1996, on the Day of Atonement, the Holy Spirit whispered this word to me: "Tell My people not to treat this current move of refreshing as an American fad.

Tell them they must stay with it long enough until it crests, until the next wave comes."

I believe that we have been experiencing a "Pentecost experience" marked by the same three signs seen in the Book of Acts, but in reverse order. We've feasted on the wine of the Spirit and have been refreshed with laughter, joy, and renewal. We have bowed our knees in humility and repentance under the fiery presence of our jealous God, the righteous King of glory. We have been lifted up in His grace as righteous, holy, and pure in His sight. Now, we are about to experience the *wind of God*, characterized by powerful supernatural gifts, supernatural encounters, and angelic intervention!

I believe that we are to be praying down supernatural encounters on a large scale. Already, some are seeing incredible divine interventions on the mission field in answer to prayer. In his article, "Praying Down Miracles," Bruce Steinbaum wrote:

> *"Researchers contend that 80 percent of the new Christians in South Asia come to Christ as a direct result of some kind of supernatural encounter.* Church planters among the Gamit people of Gujarat, India, say that membership jumped from 0 to 600,000 in ten years as a result of hundreds of miraculous healings."[2]

Mr. Steinbaum also reported in the same article that in Saudi Arabia, some Christian nurses were asked to pray for a 13-year-old girl who was dying of leukemia. According to sources familiar with her story, the girl was visited by the Lord Jesus one night, even though she knew nothing about Jesus. The next day, she announced to her astonished parent that she had met her Healer, and the entire family is now following Christ. We need to pray down supernatural encounters for cancer patients like this little girl. Pray that God will visit those who are dying of terminal diseases and will heal them. Pray that entire families and villages will follow God because of testimonies to divine visitations from on high. He also writes:

"The gospel has even penetrated Islam's most holiest city! In 1993, several Saudi believers conducted a prayer march around the periphery of Mecca, the site of the annual Haji, or pilgrimage. They asked God to establish a church in the city and reveal Himself to the two million truth-seeking pilgrims who visit the city every year to pay homage to Allah at the Ka'bah shrine. According to at least two sources, Jesus made a special guest appearance at the 1994 Haji, declaring to a group of Nigerian Muslims that He indeed was the One they were seeking.

"Some Kurds reportedly have come to Christ as a result of intercessory prayer and supernatural dreams and visions. [The Kurds live in an area some people call Kurdistan, situated in northern Iraq.] One of these new Christians was converted a few years ago in Turkish Kurdistan. An avowed atheist and the editor of an influential Marxist magazine, this man was arrested in 1981. A Christian who gave him a New Testament prayed that Jesus would reveal Himself to him in a series of dreams. At their next meeting, the man became a Christian and announced that Jesus is the One who cleanses sins.

"In Tunis, as in other parts of the Arab world, God is employing dreams, visions, and miraculous healings to draw truth-seekers to Himself. One dramatic example of this phenomenon involved a group of the Sufi Muslims in northern Africa who were chanting and dancing before Allah in hopes that he might reveal himself. They say that Jesus appeared and declared that He is the true God.

"According to the missionaries in the region, many other people living in the isolated reaches of the Sahara Desert have reported similar visions of the Lord—and they are requesting Scriptures so they can learn more about Christ.

"In Egypt, a Moslem military official said he was visited by Jesus Christ in a dream. Upon waking, he immediately sought out Christians in his unit to see if they could provide him with a copy of God's Word. Finding only one believer in his officer corps, he quietly asked if he could borrow the man's Bible. In a manner reminiscent of Annanias' reluctant ministry to Saul of Tarsus, the Christian cautiously agreed. And after several days of pouring over the Gospels, the officer became a disciple of Jesus. According to reports out of Cairo, this man has become a bold witness.

"A team of Christians reported that a Pakistani Moslem recently had a dream about a Bible descending out of heaven. While he gazed at the book in amazement, the man said he heard the voice of Jesus declaring, 'This is My Word—obey it.' Similar reports of dreams and visions are commonplace inside Pakistan.

"In Cuba a divine visitation of healing descended upon a small town about 40 miles outside the capital. Everyone who walked into the church there was healed. As news of this spread, people from all the other towns began arriving. They too were healed. Eventually people from all over the island were coming and being healed. This went on for six weeks. Tens of thousands were saved. Many churches were planted and interest in the gospel rose nationwide because everyone had heard the news. It was so powerful that even the Communist government could not deny these events. (Most of these healings were by laying on of hands—in a *Methodist* church."3

Remember, What Goes Up, Must Come Down!

Let me ask *you* the question that God asked me in the Czech Republic in January of 1993: *Have you ever considered the multidirectional dimension of prayer?* The only way souls are saved, the sick are healed, demons cast out, churches established, and the explosive supernatural gifts of God are unleashed is for people to pray. God is once again driving home this simple but vital component to true revival:

If we want to restore the expectation of the supernatural, then we must first restore the labor of love through fervent prayer on our knees! It was no accident that the Moravian believers enjoyed such effectiveness in their missionary work—they lived by one motto that we need to adopt as our own in the Church: "No one works unless someone prays." Supernatural encounters are commonplace among praying people, and myths among the prayerless. It is time for the redeemed nation of kings and priests to don their linen robes and enter the Most Holy Place to offer prayers, petitions, and intercession for all men. It is time to unleash the power of God Almighty on the earth through unleashed prayer to Heaven.

From the Eyes of a Child

Let me close out this chapter by telling you another story centering around our oldest son, Justin, when he was only seven years old. In February of 1991, I was in Atlanta, Georgia, on an intercessory mission of prayer concerning what would later be called the Gulf War. Months before the conflict ever broke out, the Lord had spoken to me to be a man of prayer through the month of February. So I kept my schedule clean to have concentrated time to be before the Lord. While I was away, Justin had an encounter of supernatural dimensions.

He was lying awake in the top bunk of his bed late one night when with his physical eyes he saw clouds enveloping his room. A brilliant throne appeared to be established in the midst of the clouds, and some creature-like things with wings, full of something that looked like fish scales, surrounded the throne. They each had different faces, and seven-year-old Justin said that one had the face of an eagle, another looked like a bull, a third looked like a lion and the fourth had the face of a man.

A ladder descended into his room and angels traipsed down the ladder—carrying fire in their hands. Single file, they would descend one at a time, stand in the room, and then proceed back up the ladder, only for another to be released to do the same. The last angel to come carried a piece of paper in his hand, and he left it on Justin's dresser. This angel climbed back up the ladder; the ladder ascended into the clouds; the clouds enfolded the throne; then everything seemed to vanish to the natural eye. Only one thing remained. A piece of angelic stationery was yet visible on Justin's dresser with a few short words imprinted upon it. Justin must have looked puzzled when he read the note. Guess what it said: *Pray for your Dad.* Amazing, isn't it? God even wants children to expect supernatural results when they pray!

Expect Great Things From God

Prayer releases Heaven's arsenal to come to the aid of man. Why not expect a supernatural God—who has not changed—to move into extraordinary ways? Who knows, when the Almighty receives the incense of your prayers, maybe a whole troupe of angels will be sent forth in response to your invitation bidding His will! Why not expect great things from God in answer to your prayers?

Endnotes

1. This prayer, of course, is a *fictional account* of what Zechariah, the priest might have said, since according to Luke 1:13 we know he had made a personal petition to the Lord. It seems likely this priest would want to make the petition from the most advantageous place at the most appropriate time—what better time under the Old Covenant than with the final offering of incense before the veil shielding the ark of the Lord and within earshot of continuous intercession from the congregation of the Lord?

2. Bruce Steinbaum, "Praying Down Miracles," an article included in the training notebook, *Fire on the Altar* compiled and published by Jim Goll of Ministry to the Nations, Nashville, Tennessee, 1995.

3. Steinbaum, "Praying Down."

Chapter 9

Restoring the ATM

(Apostolic Team Ministry)

"It's time for the "A Team" to come forth!"

"It's time for the ATM."

"It will be apostolic, authentic, abandoned Christianity."

"It will be telescopic—with prophets looking down the telescope of time and evangelists telling the good news. And it will be microscopic with pastors and administrators caring for the house."

This word came to me in a dream in the summer of 1996. I knew that this promise was that these three ministries (apostolic, telescopic, and microscopic) would cooperate together and not compete. In my heart, I thought, *Now that would be a dream!*

As I awakened from this dream, I saw a vision of a man using an ATM (automatic teller machine) card at a bank machine and receiving a withdrawal of funds. Perhaps the Lord was saying that Apostolic Team Ministry will be used to release great supplies from His storehouse for the last days' ministry. One thing is for certain at this writing: New teams and new streams are emerging every day. It is time for the prophetic to come into maturity and for true, authentic, humble apostolic ministry to emerge.

While I was in Austria ministering at a School of the Prophetic in August of 1996, the Holy Spirit awakened me in the night by hearing His external audible voice, saying:

"For the next 38½ months, I will light up one city per month with My sustained Presence—like Toronto and Pensacola."

I knew in my spirit that this word of the Lord was global in scope, and that these cities would be distributed all over the world. I also knew that some of these cities would be in out-of-the-way places, and that some of these outpourings would not be publicized widely. The names of a number mostly unfamiliar cities in foreign countries came to mind at the same time. As I pondered the words I'd heard, I realized that the time period given in the word would end somewhere on the Day of Atonement in 1999. (Now I am not predicting the second coming of Christ, the mark of the beast, or any such thing. I simply am relaying a powerful encounter to stir your faith into action.) Perhaps cities filled with spiritual fire are part of God's strategy for the harvest.

The Power of Sustained Prayer

I believe that everything we have experienced to this point is but a foretaste of what God is bringing to the Church! Up to this point, we have witnessed historic worldwide prayer events that revealed the great power of unity in prayer to God. Yet, what God revealed to our small group of intercessors on the Moravian watchtower in February of 1993 is that He is raising up *sustained unity, sustained prayer,* and *sustained intercession* in a simple pattern and style that He raised up years ago at Herrnhut. The question is obvious: If 300 people conducting sustained prayer in twos and threes for more than a century turned the world upside down 200 years ago, what can *millions* of anointed intercessors accomplish through sustained prayer in the presence of God?

Unfortunately, much of the Church has been limping along with blind eyes and crutches when it should be running to the battle! Most church congregations in the Christian world have squandered away their potential by living under the illusion that the two vital leadership gifts listed in Ephesians 4—the apostle and the prophet—somehow "passed away" somewhere between the conclusion of the Book of Acts and our day.

Gifted teachers and pastors have kept us well fed and content to learn and leave—often with little accountability for applying our ever-growing wealth of knowledge. Wise pastors brought in evangelists as often as possible and gave them orders to comfort the afflicted and afflict the comfortable, but the first love of an evangelist is on a stage or tree stump somewhere surrounded by seas of *unsaved* faces. Without the strength, foundation, and visionary leadership of apostolic ministry, our churches have lived in a perpetual state of weakness in insecurity. Deprived of the prophetic insight and God-given sense of spiritual direction and correction found in the prophet, the Church has been stumbling from one short-term goal to another, never really having or perceiving God's will for the corporate Body. Remember, where there is no vision, the people perish (see Prov. 29:18).

The Church's Condition

As a result, the Church has resembled a person whose diet is limited exclusively to heavy starch-based or fat-rich foods and sweets. The Church has become bloated from feasting exclusively on the fruits of "pastor trees" and "teacher trees," with just enough spice from from rare helpings of "evangelist trees" to provide occasional heartburn. In other words, our ignorance has deprived our corporate Body of two of five "God-ordained daily Allowances" of spiritual nutrients necessary to produce a healthy, productive, and completely equipped and spotless Bride. We are weak and malnourished because of an incomplete and unhealthy balance in our spiritual diet!

God has examined the modern-day global Body of Christ and, particularly, the North American Church, and He has found her wanting, much as He did with the churches in the Book of Revelation. She is bloated, given to much sleep and slumber, and she dislikes exercise or "the work of the ministry" in many forms. Her members have a track record of avoiding anything that requires time, effort, or personal accountability for *doing* what God commands in His Word.

> The Church has become bloated from feasting exclusively on the fruits of "pastor trees" and "teacher trees," with just enough spice from from rare helpings of "evangelist trees" to provide occasional heartburn.

"In Ten Years"

In April of 1984, my friend and revivalist, Mike Bickle, heard the voice of the Lord say something like this: "I am going to begin a new work in the earth in ten years." God commissioned him to call forth intercessory prayer in a sustained manner over the next decade and beyond. That wasn't exactly the kind of word he wanted to hear because he had just planted a new work. He was an energetic pastor in his late twenties. He didn't really want to wait ten years for a major move of God and spend much of the time in a room simply reminding God of His word, but he had no choice. God also told Mike that He was speaking to a prophetic gentleman named Bob Jones and instructed Mike to contact the man. When they met and compared notes, they discovered that God had spoken complimentary things to both men at the same time while in two different locations! Their insights became like two pieces of an interlocking puzzle.

The Lord gave Bob a revelation at that time about the Bible account of Joseph's stay in Pharoah's prison. He told Bob that it was a parable of what was going to occur over the next decade. Since God's Word declares, "Surely the Lord God does nothing unless He reveals His secret counsel to His servants the prophets" (Amos 3:7), it is appropriate for me to summarize Bob Jones' prophecy released in mid-1984. When Joseph was wrongfully thrown into Pharoah's prison for refusing the advances of Potiphar's wife, he shared his confinement with Pharoah's butler and baker, who had both been thrown in jail for offending him. Each man had a dream and Joseph accurately interpreted their dreams and predicted what would happen over the next three days.

The butler was restored to Pharoah's good favor with all of the rights and privileges of his position of service. He was released to serve in the king's presence. The baker, however, was hung high for all to see and beheaded. The birds of the air feasted on his flesh because he had served his bread with hypocrisy. (In other words, he said one thing and did another. You can stop squirming now.) Bob Jones was saying that the Lord was going to deal with the hypocritical bakers in the Kingdom, as well as with the teaching or "table" ministries in His house. He was going to deal with His household in a severe manner to cleanse the leaven of hypocrisy from our teaching ministries. At the end of these ten years, after the Lord's dealings, new little unknown servants, butlers of the king, would be released to serve at the table of the Lord and be given the awesome responsibility to serve the new wine and living bread in the King's presence. (I believe this word actually goes far beyond a single ten-year period. It describes the ongoing and progressive cleansing work of the Holy Spirit in our day and in past Church history.)

A Dramatic Fulfillment

Not long after this prophecy was released, something dramatic occurred which shocked the entire church community and outraged unsaved people around the world. Jim and Tammy Bakker were formally indicted for fraud. Many other unsavory activities also were exposed publicly at their sprawling ministry in Fort Mills, South Carolina. The greatest, most damaging exposures concerned blatant hypocrisy involving money, sexual activities, and extravagant lifestyles that brought shame to ministry and the Christian world. I only mention these things for instruction and verification of Bob Jones' prophecy, not to point a finger or be critical of anyone. God knows, we each need His mercy.

The exposure and public punishment of the Bakkers became symbolic of the cleansing work that God was doing throughout the Church. Now, ten years have gone, and this cleansing still continues. But something new entered the picture in early 1994 when God poured out His Spirit on a small church at the end of an airport runway in Toronto, Canada, and many other places. A new wine was being poured out as the Lord began to release His little servants to serve new wine and living bread in the King's presence once again.

> **One of the first signs that a great harvest**
> **is coming and has come upon us is that the**
> **prodigals are coming home from every quarter.**

Another landmark sign came exactly at the end of the ten-year period prophesied by so many vessels of God: Jimmy Bakker was released from prison. That, in itself, was a prophetic proclamation that the Lord intends to restore backsliders to the "pool of His purpose." During this same period of time, the Holy Spirit gave me some insight. One afternoon, I was watching our children playing on our swingset in our backyard. Quickly, I saw an open vision superimposed over the natural scene. With this extra dimension of spirit-sight activated, I saw a grown adult man sliding down our slide; he was positioned on his back, headfirst. In this vision, the man slid into a round swimming pool at the base of the kid's slide. I lifted up an instant request, "What does this mean?"

Immediately, a reply came within, "I will restore the backslidden man into the pool of my purpose." One of the first signs that a great harvest is coming and has come upon us is that the prodigals are coming home from every quarter. I rejoice to see Jim Bakker a restored man of humility among a people of restoration, once again proclaiming the mercy and grace of Jesus Christ. Let the prodigals return.

In the 80's, Paul Cain prophesied about a coming grand revival, still yet to come: "And the stadiums will be filled; a faceless generation (little servants) will come forth. Jesus will be magnified as the stadiums are filled as healings, miracles, and the dead are raised." This speaks of a rapid, large scale revival and harvest that only can be described as a Great Awakening in our land. In the 80's, it took a lot of courage to release a prophecy like that. Today, it is easier because we see people lining up at 4:00 in the morning just to attend evening revival services in various places and continents around the world. But a *tidal wave* of God's Presence is about to break forth.

When God unleashed His Spirit in January of 1994, it was like a "cork" had popped out of a bottle. New wine began gushing forth all over God's people. I was ministering with my intercessory co-worker, David Fitzpatrick, in a conference in Indianapolis, Indiana, in September, the day after the Day of Atonement that same year, when God began to speak to me. What I heard there relates closely to the events that occurred during this ten-year period of cleansing.

"It's Time to Begin"

I was asleep and alone in a totally dark room when I was awakened by the audible voice of the Lord. It was an unusual experience. It seemed like an angel had blown a trumpet that resonated in the room and woke me up. I sat up immediately in the bed and felt what I can only describe as "the presence of destiny" in my room. A large angel now stood at the end of my bed. The digital clock read 2:02. I sat in the bed immersed in the tangible presence of destiny for the next 30 minutes. But I had been awakened by hearing these words: "It's time to begin." The angel was what you might consider a "typical looking" angel that was dressed in white with wings, and I could see hands under the wings. The hand under one wing emerged holding a green cup filled with fresh oil.

(I thought it was wonderful because it instantly brought to mind Psalm 92:10, which says, "But Thou hast exalted my horn like that of the wild ox; I have been anointed with *fresh* oil." The Lord is dispensing fresh oil in our day. If you are stale and in need, ask Him to pour some of His anointing oil on top of you right now. Just express your hunger, desire, and need as you declare, "Over here, Lord! Right now. Remember me."

As I watched the angel holding the green cup filled with oil, he suddenly went "shhhhoooo" and left the room. I then looked over in the corner of the room a bottle was sitting. The really odd part was the label on the bottle that said, "Crisco Oil." My mind was really working at this point, and though I didn't say anything out loud, I was thinking, *Oh God, why do You always do this? Why does the prophetic always have to have this parabolic edge to it?*

Suddenly I "saw the light" and said to myself, *Oh, now I see: Jesus Christ, the **Christos**, the Anointed One.* God was saying the anointing represented by the oil wasn't being given to only one man—it was to the *Cristos company*, the "ChrisCo." He was releasing His oil for a whole company of people to come forth in His power and glory.

It's time for a kingdom of faithful butlers to arise. It is time for the cups of oil borne about in the green vessels symbolic of the priestly tribe of Levites—meaning His intercessory people, His people of praise, the people of His brilliant Presence—to arise and come forth conquering and to conquer.

I continued to gaze at this green bottle of oil that was about 12-to-18 inches tall—and at the scores of angels who began to fly out to unknown destinations. Some bore cups of the oil of anointing, others carried bottles of new wine, and all of them made the same sounds, "shhhooo, shhhhoooo," before they departed. This visitation lasted about a half an hour.

Experience has taught me not to overlook any detail in a vision—even the minor and seemingly inconsequential points. I asked the Lord, "What is the 202 about?" This was the time, 2:02, on the face of the digital clock when the visitation began. He dropped into my mind the Song of Solomon and the Book of Revelation. I turned on the light and opened my Bible to read, "Like a lily among the thorns, so is my darling..." (Song 2:2) and the passage in Revelation 2:2 praising the Ephesian church for its deeds, for its toil and perseverance, and for its test to determine false apostles.

This reminded me of the grueling ten-year period so many believers had endured in a "dry land." He had finally brought forth the cure for the spiritual boredom that had settled into the Church. He was calling us back to His royal banqueting table and bringing His butlers, His little servants, cups overflowing with the oil of gladness and anointing, priestly bottles of new wine and the joy and refreshing of the Lord.

Receiving God's Appraisal

While many believers (including myself) felt at times that we were barely "hanging on by our fingernails," the Lord had a different perspective. He is well aware of the desert conditions we endured, but He says to those who have hung on and continued, "I bless you for your godly perseverance. I say unto you that you are My lily amongst the thorns. You are My darling, My bride." Now He is releasing fresh bottles of wine and the fresh anointing of His great Presence upon us.

> **The gifts of God operating apart from the character of God are a prescription for catastrophe. God, though, is taking care of that through the cleansing and pruning periods. Now we were being freshly called back into service—hopefully wiser, humbler, and purer than we were before our affliction.**

The four little words that I received from an audible voice that day simply declared: "It's time to begin." After I'd pondered those words for several months, I began to see that God had, somewhat, put us on a "pause" mode because, as a Church, our depth of character simply didn't match up with our level of giftedness. The gifts of God operating apart from the character of God, are a prescription for catastrophe. God, though, is taking care of that through the cleansing and pruning periods. Now we were being freshly called back into service—hopefully wiser, humbler, and purer than we were before our affliction.

After that time, I was given a dream in which I saw a painter like Michaelangelo painting the arm of the Lord coming down out of clouds. Then I saw the hand and arm of a man rise up from earth the two were about to touch one another. I noticed a "baton" in the hand of the Lord as His arm extended toward earth from Heaven. I realized that the Lord was placing this baton in the hand of man as he extended his arm toward Heaven. The baton represented four "heart standards" given to Mike Bickle in a separate prophetic revelation, and to many others as well. These four heart standards were:

1. Day and night prayer
2. Extravagant giving
3. Holiness of heart
4. Unwavering (or prevailing) faith.

This dream illustrated God's longing to entrust once again into the hands of His people heart strands of purity and devotion, outreach and mercy. Now these promises have never been promised or released to just one body, one city, one denomination, or even to one "stream" in the Body of Christ. These are foundational principles and promises and prophetic declarations of the heart of God for the whole Church, the Body of Christ. God was declaring to us after a long drought, "I will restore day and night prayer. I will restore extravagant giving. I will restore a people of purity and holiness of heart. And I will restore prevailing faith amongst My people."

The Arm of the Lord

I began to search the Scriptures for references to "the arm of the Lord" and discovered some key passages:

> ...*You shall well remember what the Lord your God did to Pharaoh and to all Egypt: the great trials which your eyes saw and the signs and the wonders and the mighty hand and the outstretched arm by which the Lord your God brought you out* (Deuteronomy 7:18-19a).

Yet they are Thy people, even Thine inheritance, whom Thou hast brought out by Thy great power and by Thine outstretched arm (Deuteronomy 9:29).

And know this day that I am not speaking with your sons whom have not known and who have not seen the discipline of the Lord your God—His greatness, His mighty hand, and His outstretched arm, and His signs, and His works, which He did in the midst of Egypt to Pharaoh the king of Egypt and to all his land (Deuteronomy 11:2).

And the Lord brought us up out of Egypt with a mighty hand and an outstretched arm and with great terror and with signs and wonders (Deuteronomy 26:8).

For by their own sword they did not possess the land; and their own arm did not save them; but Thy right hand, and Thine arm, and the light of Thy presence, for Thou didst favor them (Psalm 44:3).

And the Lord will cause His voice of authority to be heard. And the descending of His arm to be seen in a fierce anger and in the flame of a consuming fire, in a cloudburst, downpour, and hailstones (Isaiah 30:30).

It appears that whenever the "arm of the Lord" reaches into our time-space world that it has something to do with signs and wonders, with deliverance, and with the brilliant display of God's power. Isaiah 52:10 tells us, "The Lord has beared His holy arm." What is the purpose of His Presence, and what is the purpose of the prophetic gifts? Isaiah 52:10 says, "In the sight of all the nations, that all the ends of the earth may *see the salvation* of our God."

Who has believed our message? And to whom has the arm of the Lord been revealed? (Isaiah 53:1).

I have made the earth, the men and the beasts which are on the face of the earth by My great power and by My out stretched arm, and I will give it to the one who is pleasing in My sight (Jeremiah 27:5).

The "arm of the Lord" symbolically represents strength, power, the demonstration of God's right to both to discipline and to deliver in the Scriptures. During a time of extended ministry in the Los Angeles area, I went with Lou Engle, pastor of prayer at Harvest Rock Church in Pasadena, California, and some other friends on an expedition to do some on-site locational praying. We prayed at the original site of the Azusa Street outpouring and also at the little house nearby where the Holy Spirit first baptized believers before the little group moved to the Azusa Street location. Then we headed for a place called Pisgah, which was another center of Pentecostal renewal.

Calling Forth the Arm of the Lord

Finally, we visited Angelos Temple, the founding church of the Four Square International Church established by Aimee Semple MacPherson in the 1920s. That church and Aimee Semple MacPherson's ministry were very powerful in that day. After we went through a little museum area and examined some of the documents on display, our wonderful host took our party of eight right into the auditorium to pray.

Once we reached the auditorium and settled in to pray, our host left us alone in that incredible place. We saw a beautiful grand piano sitting on the platform. Someone mentioned that Aimee Semple MacPherson played it during her services. At that point, my dear missionary friend, Mark Young from Thailand, sat down at the piano and began to play in the spirit. Then, we just waited quietly in the Presence of the Lord in this wonderful auditorium that had played host and witness to countless miracles, signs, and wonders in this century.

While we waited on the Lord, I sat down on a step leading to the platform, just soaking in the sweet Presence of the Lord in that place. Finally, I just lay down on the platform before the Presence of the Lord. When we first came in, we were struck by the perfect acoustics of the auditorium. It had a high-domed ceiling. You could speak from the stage without a microphone, and the sound resonated around the building with total clarity.

While Mark played on the piano, I began to pray out loud as I basked in God's Presence. Then I *really* began to pray. Finally, I began then to prophesy as something started to rise up within me. I moved into a place of prophetic declaration, and began to prophesy:

> "I will restore the sacred altar. I will restore My fire upon My altar. I will restore. I am going to bring forth the arm of the Lord. I am going to release apostolic restoration ministries. I am going to restore the four faces of My gospel. I am going to release the four faces of My living creatures that are around My throne. Let the arm of the Lord come forth!"

Then I prophesied the restoration of the four-square gospel of the King, the Savior, the Baptizer, and the Healer; and of the ARM—the Apostolic Restoration Ministries. It is time for the apostolic restoration ministries to begin.

The Prophetic Sets the Table

It has been prophesied for years that the prophetic would set a table for the apostolic. I must declare boldly that it is time to begin. I am not giving definitions of what the "apostolic" is because that is not my purpose or expertise. Nevertheless, it is time for apostolic restoration ministries to come forth.

I continued to pray, prophesy, and release prophetic declarations. Finally I said out loud, "Oh may the altar of the Lord be restored!" Suddenly, I felt the floor start to rise underneath me out of the floor! No, I wasn't having a dream or vision, and I wasn't in a trance. An altar began to rise out of the floor that must have measured three feet wide by six feet long. It kept rising, and I kept prophesying: "The altar of the Lord is coming. Fire is coming on My altar." (I'm telling you a prophetic event that really happened.)

A Living Sacrifice

I couldn't help but notice the significance of my position on the rising altar while I prophesied life and restoration. God is looking for a living sacrifices according to Romans 12: "...present your bodies a living and holy sacrifice, acceptable to God, which is your spiriual service of worship" (Rom. 12:1b). *We* are the sacrifice that is well pleasing and acceptable in God's sight. He is jealous for us, and He wants us to present our whole being on His altar—with spirit, soul, and body.

When the altar reached the end of its track, I just kind of slid down slowly until the altar was right behind me, as other people in the group watched. I remained in that place declaring in prophetic proclamation,

"I will restore the fame of My great name in all the earth. I will restore the four faces of the gospel. I will restore My truth of being Savior, Baptizer, and Healer. I will release My four faces and My living creatures. I will bring forth, and I shall roll up My sleeve, and I shall bear My holy right arm. I will restore the ancient altar. I will bring forth My holy right arm."

Things will probably end up looking different from what we expect right now, but the Lord is going to breathe fresh prophetic and apostolic teaching and revelation on the ancient discipline of day and night prayer. He is going to release a new understanding of extravagant giving and a new place of holiness of heart. The fire of God is an all-consuming fire that can dry up cancer or convict men of their sins.

Apostolic Restoration Ministries

What is the arm of the Lord? It is a symbol of the Lord's strength and power. It is the demonstration of God's ability to both discipline and deliver. It is likely that His arm refers to apostolic restoration ministries or apostolic team ministries in this great revival. But even more accurately, the arm of the Lord usually refers to Jesus Christ Himself: "And I will bear My holy right arm." You know, this is not about us. It isn't about anointed men and women. This is all about Jesus—the Sacrificial Lamb receiving the reward of His suffering. Let's make our focus clear.

This is not about us. This is about our wonderful Messiah, Jesus Christ, our transcendent Majesty.

This is about the power of His great Presence. If you recall, I mentioned how God once told me, "I am going to teach you to release the highest weapon of spiritual warfare. I am going to teach you to release the brilliance of My great Presence." What is the highest weapon of spiritual warfare? Why, it's God, Himself.

> **What is the arm of the Lord? It is a symbol of the Lord's strength and power. It is the demonstration of God's ability to both discipline and deliver. It is likely that His arm refers to apostolic restoration ministries or apostolic team ministries in this great revival.**

The Lord has been looking for broken people. He has been looking for a humble people who can be trusted with God's treasure because they know that it's not them—it is Jesus. According to Psalm 110:2, the Lord is seeking them out to place His scepter of kingly authority and power into their hands to rule over their enemies out of Zion (God's abiding presence). Let the "A team" come forth. Let the arm of the lord be stretched out! It's time for a faceless people to emerge, a generation of little butlers whose passion is the exaltation of this one Man, God and King—Christ Jesus, the Lord.

Chapter 10

The Day of the
Watch Has Come

"I will restore the ancient tool, the Watch of the Lord, that has been used and will be used again to change the expression of Christianity across the face of the earth."

This final chapter represents the most difficult task of this book. Why? Because a burden has been placed on my heart to break the vile curse that has overcome and contaminated the Church and the ministry since the days when James echoed the teachings of Jesus and admonished believers:

*But prove yourselves **doers** of the word, and not **merely hearers** who delude themselves. For if anyone is a hearer of the word and not a doer, he is like a man who looks at his natural face in a mirror; for once he has looked at himself and gone away, he has immediately **forgotten what kind of person he was** (James 1:22-24).*

Some years have passed since the Lord told me, "It is time to begin." Since then the fire of God has fallen in countless places across the globe (including supposedly "impregnable" places such as Japan and Mecca). My burden is to awaken the "saved and redeemed" and remind them *who they are!* Only then will

144 The Lost Art of Intercession

they begin to obey and, in turn, pray for the salvation of the lost in God's great harvest. Oddly enough, this has often proven to be the most difficult group to reach!

Since God ignited my burden for the Watch of the Lord at Herrnhut, the site of the great Moravian prayer watch, it is no accident that He has sent me to draw from their deep pool of wisdom again and again along my journey. The Day of the Watch has come. The words of the Rev. John Greenfield, the great Moravian evangelist and author, ring as true today as they did 70 or more years ago:

> "Prayer always precedes Pentecost. The Book of Acts describes many outpourings of The Holy Spirit, but never apart from prayer. In our own day the great Welsh and Korean revivals were preceded by months, if not years, of importunate and united praying. Hence the supreme importance of the prayer meeting, for it is 'the power house of the Church.' "[1]

In previous chapters, I mentioned that the Lord told me, "I will restore Pentecost." Many people think that is an odd or even heretical statement. "After all, Pentecost happened once and for all." I also spoke of a "Second Pentecost" coming to the land, but while I was completing some research for this final chapter, I discovered a better way to describe this work of God: He is sending yet *another* Pentecost!

The Moravians, and many supposedly "fundamental evangelical" leaders believed and prayed for the same thing and received it! The only way to spread fire is to catch fire! Theology never saved anyone—only a personal experience with a living Savior can do it. Theology never launched a worldwide revival. In every case, it took a fresh revelation of the living Savior to ignite the world with fire from Heaven. Before you can participate in the Watch of the Lord, you must offer yourself as a living sacrifice on the altar of God and let Him baptize you afresh in His holy fire!

D.L. Moody, one of America's most revered evangelists and conservative church leaders had this to say about the Holy Spirit in one of the last sermons he preached in his life:

> "See how He came on the day of Pentecost! It is not carnal to pray that He may come again and that the place be shaken. I believe Pentecost was but a specimen day. I think the Church has made this woeful mistake that Pentecost was a miracle never to be repeated. I have thought too that Pentecost was a miracle that is not to be repeated. I believe now if we looked on Pentecost as a specimen day and began to pray, we should have the old Pentecostal fire here in Boston."[2]

God is restoring the fire of the Holy Spirit to His people so *we* will restore the fire of prayer on His altar of incense and release the glory of God on the earth! Look at the striking parallels between the outpouring of the Holy Spirit on people of prayer in Jerusalem, and on another people of prayer 17 centuries later in Herrnhut, Saxony!

> "Verily the history of the Moravian Church confirms the doctrine of the great American evangelist [D.L. Moody] as to the need and possibility of the baptism with the Holy Ghost. The spiritual experiences of the Moravian Brethren two centuries ago bear a striking resemblance to the Pentecostal power and results in the days of the Apostles.

> "The company of believers both at Jerusalem and Herrnhut numbered fewer than three hundred souls. Both congregations were, humanly speaking, totally devoid of worldly influence, wisdom, power and wealth. Their enemies called them 'unlearned and ignorant.' Their best friend described them in the following language:

> " 'Ye see your calling, brethren, how that not many wise men after the flesh, not many mighty, not many noble are called; but God hath chosen the foolish things of the world to confound the wise, and God hath chosen the weak

things of the world to confound the things which are mighty; and the base things of the world, and things which are despised, hath God chosen, yea, and things which are not, to bring to naught things that are, that no flesh should glory in His presence' (1 Cor. 1:26-28).

"On both these small and weak congregations God poured out His Holy Spirit and endued them with power from on high. At once these believers, naturally timid and fearful, were transformed into flaming evangelists. Supernatural knowledge and power seemed to possess them. 'Mouth and wisdom' were given them which 'none of their adversaries were able to gainsay or resist.' "[3]

The same God who engineered this miracle in Jerusalem and in Herrnhut in the 1700s appears determined to do the same across the earth before the dawn of the millennium! God is not interested in "corporate assent" to the principle of revival—He demands personal surrender, commitment, and sold-out service in prayer and public witness to His glory!

When the people of God dare to surrender to the Holy Spirit of God and then live lives of continuous consecrated prayer, they will display an infectious joy that will draw the lost to them again and again in divine appointments of destiny. An editorial in the *Wachovia Moravian* described a "typical Moravian" affected by the Pentecostal outpouring of that day:

"There was a Countess several generations ago who had led what the world calls a very merry life. She was highly situated in society, connected in close friendship with kings and emperors and princes. She was a welcome centre on brilliant occasions of dance and festivity in view of her brilliant gifts and witty conversation, and yet she became afflicted with an incurable melancholy. None of her amusements and recreations satisfied her any longer and everything before her and around her seemed dark indeed.

"Under the old custom of measuring shoes for the feet of their wearers, an humble Moravian shoemaker was one day invited into her presence. As he opened the door, she was struck by the remarkable cheerfulness which shone forth from his face. She watched him closely while he knelt at his humble task of measuring for the shoes and was deeply impressed by the unaffected happiness written upon his very looks. She was led to say to him, 'You seem to be a very happy man.' 'Yes,' he said, 'I am very happy all the time.' 'You are very different from me,' the high-born lady said. 'I am just as miserable as anybody could be. Would you mind telling me what makes you so happy?' 'No,' the Moravian shoemaker said, 'I'll be glad to tell you. Jesus has forgiven my sins. He forgives me every day and He loves me and that makes me happy through all the hours.'

"The job was finished and the man went away. But the Countess thought over what he said. Thought led to prayer and prayer to conviction and conviction swiftly introduced her into a joyful faith in the shoemaker's Saviour. She became a witness for Christ among titled people and especially at the court of the Emperor of Russia, Alexander I, her intimate friend."[4]

God's Intention

Matthew Henry wrote, "When God intends great mercy for His people, the first thing He does is to set them a praying."[5] God intends to cover the earth with His glory and with a flood of mercy and grace. But first God must wake His sleeping giant, the Church. It is time for you and I to shake the world for Christ from our places of prevailing prayer! We can no longer afford to hear the urgent word of the Lord and walk away passively. The call is the same regardless of what title or flavor adorns the sign over the door of our place of worship.

I am compelled in the spirit to urge you to prayer. After I ministered a message on "The Watch of the Lord" in Mobile,

Alabama, I returned home to discover that I had been sent a very beautiful framed picture in the mail. This gracious giver had no idea what effect that picture would have on my life. I personally believe that this picture constitutes *the highest prophetic word that I have ever been given in my life!* It is a picture of monumental proportions in front of my eyes.

The picture depicts a great city encircled by a protective wall. A hill rises on one side and coming over that hill were hundreds of invaders on horses. The picture also depicts a watchman on the wall—*a watchman who has fallen asleep.* The trumpet normally used to signal the approach of danger lay useless beside the slumbering watchman. Meanwhile, the enemy drew closer and closer to the defenseless city.

> **Jesus warned us eleven times to "be on the watch, be on the alert, wake up, and watch out that no one deceives you." Too many of us have stopped listening and stopped caring.**

When I first unwrapped this picture, I thought, "Lord, this is wonderful. This is a great gift." Then I read the verse inscribed below the scene, and suddenly I wasn't as excited as before. The verse was Ezekiel 33:6, which says, "But if the watchman sees the sword coming and does not blow the trumpet, and the people are not warned, and a sword comes and takes a person from them, he is taken away in his iniquity; *but his blood I will require from the watchman's hand.*"

I avoid using this Scripture passage in a legalistic or condemning manner, but it made the "sobriety of God" sink into my inner being. I know that I am called to be a watchman of the Lord. I don't want to fulfill the failure depicted in that picture. Jesus warned us 11 times to "be on the watch, be on the alert, wake up, and watch out that no one deceives you." Too many of us have stopped listening and stopped caring.

God is calling His watchmen—every blood-washed saint and redeemed king and priest—in groups of twos or threes to come together on the wall. He is calling forth the ancient tools to bring salvation to our generation. *Do you believe dead men's bones can live again?*

I believe dead men's bones *will* live again. I believe that the same Spirit who kept the promises of God for generations in the past is waiting for us to enter into the Holy of holies for our time and our generation! There is only one path for you to take if you have received and believed the message of this book: You need to be possessed. (Don't close your mind and the pages of this book—this is a Bible concept!) God wants you to be possessed with His Spirit in the same way Gideon was! The Amplified Bible says:

> *But the Spirit of the Lord clothed Gideon with Himself and took possession of him, and he blew a trumpet, and [the clan of] Abiezer was gathered to him* (Judges 6:34 AMP).

Get Possessed!

God is waiting for a people to get possessed. He wants a people who will literally be clothed with God Himself, and will blow the trumpet with holy boldness as watchmen on the wall. Are you willing to be possessed? Are you ready for a radical change of clothes?

I have always liked Gideon because I can really identify with him. He was minding his own business and working in his own field when somebody (an angel of the Lord) tapped him on the shoulder and said, "Hey you, mighty man of courage, God wants to use you."

I can imagine Gideon looking around and saying, "Who in the world are you talking to, buddy?" (See Judges 6:11-17.) As it was with Gideon, God's analysis of our potential is vastly different from our own. God is looking for a people who understand how small they are and how great He is. Then, He just loves to turn the tables on all the naysayers and contenders by possessing us and taking residence within us.

Gideon's father was not a righteous man because he had built up the high places in honor of idols and false gods. Everyone nearby came to the site to conduct their devilish rites of idolatry. In the same way, our nation can no longer can be called a "Christian nation" because we've turned aside to the idols of self, personal pleasure, and rebellion. Nevertheless, the Spirit of the Lord gave Gideon the task of tearing down the very high places that his father had built! Gideon decided to obey the angel's command, but he was wondering, *I'm not quite so sure because you're talking about dividing my own household here.* He was so afraid of his father's reaction to the destruction of the high places that he did it at night.

Gideon's clumsy attempt to hide his deed didn't work, evidently because one of the ten men who helped him decided to tell all (Judg. 6:29). When the angry idol worshipers confronted Gideon's father, Joash, he said prophetically, "If he [Baal] is a god, let him contend for himself because someone has torn down his altar" (Judg. 6:31b). Although Joash intended for this statement to be a curse on the guilty man, it set up a test of truth similar to the confrontation of Elijah with the priests of Baal when God's fire consumed all of the priests of Baal as well as Elijah's water-soaked altar and sacrifice. In the ancient traditions of that day, it was understood that anyone who dared to break the curse would themselves receive a penalty in their own lives.

Gideon faced some serious problems that day. You may be facing some obstacles in your life that make commitment to the Lord's call seem impossible or even suicidal. The Lord is looking tirelessly for a people who will overcome small mentalities, insecurities, and fears to allow Him to take control. When you allow God to clothe you with Himself, when you "put on Christ," you will have a totally different perspective of the obstacles challenging you today. Too many Christians are afraid to step out of their own comfort zones and venture into places that the world (and many Christians) call "too radical."

God's Reward System

God has a reward for people who dare to step out on the limb of faith and just keep on going. There was a reward for Gideon. He counted the cost of obeying God's command. He had to face his paralyzing fear of reprisal if he dared to come against his own father's household. Gideon counted the cost and stepped over the line into obedience to God anyway. He was still "human" enough to do the deed in the dark of night, but the point is that he obeyed. Once he stepped out, the Bible says that he "waxed strong" He became stronger!

Look what happens to the man who steps forward for "more" of God in his life. The Bible says, "So the Spirit of the Lord came upon Gideon; and he blew a trumpet, and the Abiezrites were called together to follow him" (Judg. 6:34). I was in a prayer conference in Canada several years ago after I had spent three solid months seeking God. Many of those days were spent praying in tongues for four to six hours a day. This trip to Canada was my "first time out" after three months of prayer. I went into a place of intercession there in Canada, and the Holy Spirit illuminated this verse in Judges chapter six. He put on my heart to read the passage from the Amplified Version.

As usual when I go into intercession and travail, I was sitting on the floor of the room. When I turned to Judges 6:34 in my wife's Amplified Bible, I read these words with astonishment: "But the Spirit of the Lord *clothed Gideon with Himself* and *took possession of him*, and he blew a trumpet, and [the clan of] Abiezer was gathered to him (Josh. 6:34 AMP).

> We hear a lot of talk about people being possessed
> by the devil, but I have something shocking to tell
> you: *God is looking for a people that He can possess.*

I've got a word from the Lord for you: *Be possessed.* We hear a lot of talk about people being possessed by the devil, but I have something shocking to tell you: *God is looking for a people that He can possess.* He wants to do more than legally own us because

He purchased us with His blood. He also wants to experientially *have us.* I don't know about you, but I want to be possessed by and with God. I want literally to be clothed with Him. I urge you to let God come upon you, to be possessed of God.

Look at the evidence in the Bible. When the Spirit of the Lord came upon or possessed Gideon, he was changed into a new man! He was no longer just a little puny guy with a mouth full of excuses about how poor his tribe was. He was possessed by God. He dared to sound the trumpet and, suddenly, to his surprise, thousands of people were suddenly willing to follow him! One moment he's a farmer in a barley field. The next moment he gets possessed by God and sees 32,000 armed men come at his simple command ready for a battle to the death with the Midianites who held the Jews in slavery! That must have been some day.

Making the Team!

God's work of transformation didn't stop there. He was out to raise up a true leader, not just a one-time, soon-to-be-forgotten hero. When God came down to examine Gideon's newly found troops, He told Gideon, "Hey, buddy, there are too many of them out there. In fact, there are so many of them coming with you that *if you win,* the men will look at themselves and say, 'We did it.' "

And the Lord said to Gideon, "The people who are with you are too many for Me to give Midian into their hands, lest Israel become boastful, saying, 'My own power has delivered me.' Now therefore come, proclaim in the hearing of the people, saying, 'Whoever is afraid and trembling, let him return and depart from Mount Gilead.' So 22,000 people returned, but 10,000 remained (Judges 7:2-3).

This scene was similar to like the public basketball tryouts for the Los Angeles Lakers or Chicago Bulls basketball teams. A whole bunch of people answered Gideon's call, but only a third made the first cut for people who were fearful and afraid. Over two-thirds of Gideon's miracle crowd left. (This statistical percentage probably would hold true today.)

Then the Lord said to Gideon, "The people are still too many; bring them down to the water and I will test them for you there. Therefore it shall be that he of whom I say to you, 'This one shall go with you,' he shall go with you; but everyone of whom I say to you, 'This one shall not go with you,' he shall not go." So he brought the people down to the water. And the Lord said to Gideon, "You shall separate everyone who laps the water with his tongue, as a dog laps, as well as everyone who kneels to drink." Now the number of those who lapped, putting their hand to their mouth, was 300 men; but all the rest of the people kneeled to drink water (Judges 7:4-6).

Twenty-two thousand of Gideon's surprise helpers were afraid. That's easy to understand. That left him with ten thousand armed men for the battle. Then came "Cut number two." God said, "Send them down to the river for a drink water. And Gideon, I want you watch them while they do it. Whoever gets down on both knees send him home. But whoever laps the water like a dog, keep him. I can run with them."

I wonder if Gideon thought something like, *Sure God, yeah, right.* It doesn't matter, because Gideon's actions spoke louder. He sent 10,000 armed men stampeding down to the river for a drink, and 9,700 of these football-player types got down on both knees and put their faces down into the water to really go for it. The problem was that when these guys were down on both knees with half of their faces in the water, the only thing that they could see was their own reflection. Less than one man out of every ten made this final cut, leaving Gideon with only 300 out of his original instant army of 32,000 men. He felt good about it, though, because these men met God's main requirement for battle fitness: "Look for those who will lap the water like a dog."

I don't know if you have ever watched a dog eat or drink, but dogs always *watch* while they eat or drink. They keep one eye on the water bowl and one eye on the terrain to see who is approaching. A dog doesn't bury himself in self-containment. It sounds just like the message of Jesus in the Gospels to me. Four times He told us, "Do not be afraid" (that's the first cut). Four times He said, "Endure, stand" (that's the second cut). A full 11 times the Lord commanded us: "Watch" (the final and most important requirement for battle).

Nehemiah's Tools

When Nehemiah the prophet risked all to rebuild the wall of Jerusalem in occupied territory filled with violent enemies, the first thing he did was to establish watchmen on the walls. In fact, everyone who worked on the wall was both workman and watchman, builder and soldier. They would work with a trowel in one hand and a spear in the other. God is quickly setting things into place to build His Church in a quick work. Again, this building project takes place in temporarily occupied territory surrounded by violent and desperate enemies. The first thing God is setting in place is "the Watch of the Lord." You've made the first two "cuts." Now He has led you to the river for a test. Will you look at yourself, at what you have, and be content with what you see? Or will you eagerly receive His gifts today but carefully keep a watch for the Master's signals and the enemies schemes?

What are the rewards for these labors? If you could ask the Moravians this question, they would instantly answer: "To win for the Lamb that was slain the reward of His sufferings." The prayers of the "possessed" are more powerful than any of us know. A German historian named Dr. Warneck wrote in his book, *Protestant Missions*, "This small Church [the Moravians] in twenty years *called into being* more missions than the whole Evangelical Church has done in two centuries."[6]

The work of the Holy Spirit was so complete and deep in the people at Herrnhut that they literally began to live out in microcosm the plan of God for His spotless Bride when He returns! Listen to the words John Wesley wrote after visiting Herrnhut in August of 1738, as recorded by Moravian historian Rev. John Greenfield:

" 'God has given me at length,' he wrote to his brother Samuel, 'the desire of my heart. I am with a Church whose conversation is in Heaven; in whom is the mind that was in Christ, and who so walk as He walked.' In his journal he wrote: 'I would gladly have spent my life here; but my Master called me to labour in another part of His vineyard. O when shall this Christianity cover the earth, as the waters cover the sea?' "[7]

On a Worldwide Scale

God fully intends to do on a worldwide scale what He did more than 200 years ago among a divided group of believers from diverse backgrounds. He is out to raise up a Church, a nation of kings and priests, whose determination is to know nothing among men save Jesus Christ and Him crucified, whose theology has become Christology, and whose creed was in one word, the "Cross."

Are you willing to be "possessed for prayer?" Will you yield yourself as a living sacrifice this very day so that God can clothe you with Himself and conduct warfare for souls? Little keys open big doors. What goes up must come down!

The key to fulfillment and fruitfulness in your life is found in one word of eternal significance: "**Yes.**" Your commission is clear: As a king and priest cleansed by the blood of Jesus, your lifelong calling is to offer the fire and incense of prayer, praise, worship, and intercession to the Most High God and to intercede on behalf of this lost and dying generation.

> **The key to fulfillment and fruitfulness in your life is found in one word of eternal significance: "Yes."**

Allow the Spirit of Pentecost to fall on you again in all of His fire and glory. Find those of like mind who also have discovered the secrets and power of God's altar of prayer. Join with one or two others to harmonize your requests to God as you restore the Watch of the Lord in your area. Work with your pastor or church members to raise up a "house of prayer for all nations" that truly fulfills the desire of God.

Pray for the harvest, for workers of the harvest. Seek the face of Him who bared His right Arm in Christ Jesus and redeemed you from the kingdom of darkness. Then, do anything and everything that He tells you with all of your heart. The Moravians discovered the secret place of power called prayer. They also lived out another secret of effective Christian living—that *all men and women* are ministers of the gospel of Jesus and stewards of a sacred hope that must be trumpeted to hurting people at every occasion. It is time to mount the wall of the Lord. It is time to light the watch fires and restore the lost art of intercession, the ancient tool of the Lord, to the Church of the Lord. Let it begin!

A Prayer of Consecration

Here I am, Lord. Possess me with your Holy Life. Teach me to release the highest weapon of spiritual warfare— the brillance of your great Presence. Let the fire of your hot love burn on the altar of my heart. Let there be fire on my altar and may it never go out. Count me in. Sign me up as a watchman on your wall. Restore the lost art of intercession. Restore the power and the passion of the watch of the Lord. For Christ's namesake. Amen.

Endnotes

1. Rev. John Greenfield, *Power From on High Or the Two Hundreth Anniversary of the Great Moravian Revival 1727-1927* (Atlantic City, New Jersey; The World Wide Revival Prayer Movement, 1927), 23.

2. Greenfield, *Power*, 13-14.

3. Greenfield, *Power*, 16-17.

4. Greenfield, *Power*, 54-55.

5. Greenfield, *Power*, 23.

6. Greenfield, *Power*, 19.

7. Greenfield, *Power*, 67.

RESTORING THE LOST ARTS OF INTERCESSION

MTTN is now offering Jim Goll's excellently prepared Study Notes on this important topic. Great for personal use, prayer groups, sermons, or Bible studies. Use these notes with the tape series or simply alone.

RTLAI...**$8.00**

CONSECRATED CONTEMPLATIVE PRAYER

These lessons bring us understanding from the truths of Christian mystics of the past. Includes materials on Ministry of Fasting, Contemplative Prayer, and Quieting Our Souls Before God. Great for developing a deeper life with God.

CCP.. **$8.00**

WAR IN THE HEAVENLIES

Carefully prepared materials on Spiritual Warfare. Subjects range from The Fall of Lucifer to Dealing with Territorial Spirits, The Weapons of Our Warfare, High Praises, The Blood Sprinkled Seven Times, and other great messages.

SNWH...**$8.00**

STIRRING UP COMPASSIONATE, PROPHETIC INTERCESSION

Study Notes on subjects of travail, weeping, high praises, laughing, prophetic intercession, and much more. Jim's favorite!

SUCPI...**$8.00**

BLUEPRINTS FOR PRAYER

Here we find detailed outlines on Confessing Generational Sins, Reminding God of His Word, Praying for Those in Authority, Praying On Site With Insight, etc. Thorough and precise. Get exposed to the many different blueprints of prayer.

BPFP...**$8.00**

RELEASING SPIRITUAL GIFTS

Lessons on the Nine Gifts of the Spirit, How Gifts Are Received, How the Holy Spirit Moves, and other themes that will equip you to do the stuff!

RSG...**$8.00**

STUDY NOTES SERIES

FOUNDATIONS FOR PROPHETIC MINISTRY
The first of a series on Prophetic Study Notes, Jim brings you three sections on Prophetic Foundations, Equipment, and Expressions. Basic and yet gripping in its content.
FFPM..$8.00

PROPHETIC MATURATION
Study Notes on maturing in the prophetic. Helpful, concise, and enlightening. Topics on Calling, Training, and Commissioning, The Seer and the Prophet, and more. Character Issues and Relational Dynamics are discussed at length.
SNPM..$8.00

UNDERSTANDING SUPERNATURAL ENCOUNTERS
Includes materials on Keys to the Supernatural, Understanding the Anointing, Angelic Encounters, Levels of Supernatural Visions, Trances, and more.
USNE.. $8.00

HANDLING DREAMS, VISIONS AND REVELATIONS
These materials include Tools, for Interpreting Revelation, Journaling, Dream Language, Judging Revelation, and more.
HDVR..$8.00

EQUIPPING BELIEVERS FOR PERSONAL MINISTRY
These Study Notes will help you lay a proper foundation for personal ministry. The Five Stage Healing Model, Ministering the Baptism in the Holy Spirit, Walking in the Spirit of Counsel, Breaking Emotional Bondage, Healing the Wounded Spirit,and Releasing a Word of Knowledge, are a few of the subjects carefully covered.
EBFPM..$8.00

POWER AND ANOINTING FOR DELIVERANCE
These Study Notes combine lessons on the Anointing, The Ministry of Deliverance, and Curses: Causes and Cures. In detail style.
PAFD..$8.00

JIM'S BEST ALBUMS

DYNAMIC PRAYER / INTERCESSION

CONTEMPLATIVE PRAYER
A4CPG..$21.00

QUIETING OUR SOULS BEFORE GOD
A3QOS..$16.00

SPIRIT OF TRAVAIL
A2SOT..$11.00

REVELATION OF THE POWER OF PRAISE
A2RPP..$11.00

EXPOSING SATAN'S INFLUENCE UPON US
A3ESI...$16.00

BORN FOR BATTLE
A4BBB..$21.00

FIRE ON THE ALTAR
A4FOA..$21.00
VIDEO..(940624v16)................................$17.00

EQUIPPING IN THE PROPHETIC

DREAM LANGUAGE
A2DLG..$11.00

LEVELS OF SUPERNATURAL VISIONS
A2LSU..$11.00
VIDEO...(961004VB-1).............................$17.00

INTERPRETING DREAMS AND REVELATION
A2IDR...$11.00

VARIETIES OF PROPHETIC ANOINTINGS
A3VPA..$16.00

ANGELIC ENCOUNTERS
A4AES..$21.00

TRANCES: A BIBLICAL VIEW
A2TBV..$11.00

SINGLE TAPES BY JIM W. GOLL

DYNAMIC PRAYER / INTERCESSION

FROM PRAYER TO HIS PRESENCE
FF20D..$5.00
VIDEO...........(950620V12)............................$17.00

LISTENING, WAITING, AND WATCHING
EB26D..$5.00

WISDOM ISSUES FOR INTERCESSORS
GF20D..$5.00

PRAYING FOR ISRAEL
GK09A...$5.00

**PRAYING YOUR FAMILY
INTO GOD'S FAMILY**
FF25A...$5.00

THE MANTLE OF PRAYER
FA28A...$5.00

REMINDING GOD OF HIS WORD
B100A...$5.00

EQUIPPING IN THE PROPHETIC

RELEASING CREATIVITY
GF22B..$5.00
VIDEO.......(960713V7)..............................$17.00

THE DECEPTION OF THE ANOINTING
EF15A..$5.00

**SEVEN EXPRESSIONS
OF THE PROPHETIC SPIRIT**
BG14B..$5.00
VIDEO.......(961004V7)..............................$17.00

HEARING GOD'S VOICE
FK01A...$5.00

HOW TO RECEIVE REVELATION
GC16A..$5.00

JUDGING REVELATION
AC06A..$5.00

**PITS AND PINNACLES OF
PROPHETIC MINISTRY**
FF17B..$5.00
VIDEO.........(950617V8)..............................$17.00

MICHAL ANN GOLL

It's finally here! In these new 2 Tapes by Jim and Michal Ann they tell the stories of the visitations of the Holy Spirit and the lessons learned through these powerful encounters. Michal Ann intimately shares from the depth of her heart the treasures the Lord has freely given to her.

VISITATIONS IN THE NIGHT
A2VIN..**$11.00**

WOMEN OF COURAGE
HD5F...**$5.00**

ANNIE GET YOUR GUN
GE03A...**$5.00**

NO MORE FEAR!
GE11A...**$5.00**

CASTING OFF EVERY WEIGHT
A2CEW..**$11.00**

BURDEN OF THE HEART
HD4D...**$5.00**

WOMEN IN THE PROPHETIC
DG24B...**$5.00**
Video.(960713V10).................................**$17.00**

LOVELINESS OF LONELINESS.
EC05G...**$5.00**

FIRE ON THE ALTAR
Intercessory Study Manual

Fire On The Altar is a beautifully designed three - ring binder with section dividers. Each article is labeled according to its section. Articles are written by Jim W. Goll and other teachers, intercessors, and leaders in the Body of Christ to equip and inspire you. Reprinted and Revised.

Special Edition..............................**$20.00**
Originally $29.99
FOTA..**$20.00**

ORDER FORM

Method of Payment: ❑ Visa ❑ Mastercard ❑ Check

Expiration Date _____

Account _____ _____ _____ _____

QTY	ITEM	DESCRIPTION	TOTAL
		Merchandise Total	
		Shipping & Handling	
		Total Amount Due	

Your Name _____

Address _____

City _____ State_____ Zip_____

Phone No. _____

Shipping Cost:
Orders up to $10.00..................$3.95
$10.01 to $20.00......................$4.95
$20.0 to $50.00........................$5.95
$50.01 to $100.00....................$6.95
Orders over $100, add 10% for shipping.

Send your information with check made payable to:

**Ministry to the Nations
P.O. Box 338
Antioch, TN. 37011-0338**

Or fax / credit card orders to:
(615) 365-4408

All contributions to MTTN are tax-deductible as allowable by law.

Please allow 2 to 4 weeks for delivery on all orders.

See us on the Internet: **http://www.reapernet.com/mttn**

Destiny Image
Revival Books

LET NO ONE DECEIVE YOU
by Dr. Michael L. Brown.
No one is knowingly deceived. Everyone assumes it's "the other guy" who is off track. So when people dispute the validity of current revivals, how do you know who is right? In this book Dr. Michael Brown takes a look at current revivals and at the arguments critics are using to question their validity. After examining Scripture, historical accounts of past revivals, and the fruits of the current movements, Dr. Brown comes to a logical conclusion: God's Spirit is moving. *Let No One Deceive You!*
Paperback Book, 312p. ISBN 1-56043-693-X (6" X 9") Retail $10.99

THE GOD MOCKERS
And Other Messages From the Brownsville Revival
by Stephen Hill.
Hear the truth of God as few men have dared to tell it! In his usual passionate and direct manner, Evangelist Stephen Hill directs people to an uncompromised Christian life of holiness. The messages in this book will burn through every hindrance that keeps you from going further in God!
Paperback Book, 182p. ISBN 1-56043-691-3 Retail $8.99

IT'S TIME
by Richard Crisco.
"We say that 'Generation X' does not know what they are searching for in life. But we are wrong. They know what they desire. We, as the Church, are the ones without a revelation of what they need." It is time to stop entertaining our youth with pizza parties and start training an army for God. Find out in this dynamic book how the Brownsville youth have exploded with revival power...affecting the surrounding schools and communities!
Paperback Book, 140p. ISBN 1-56043-690-5 Retail $8.99

A TOUCH OF GLORY
by Lindell Cooley.
This book was written for the countless "unknowns" who, like Lindell Cooley, are being plucked from obscurity for a divine work of destiny. Here Lindell, the worship leader of the Brownsville Revival, tells of his own journey from knowing God's hand was upon him to trusting Him. The key to personal revival is a life-changing encounter with the living God. There is no substitute for a touch of His glory.
Paperback Book, 182p. ISBN 1-56043-689-1 Retail $8.99

Available at your local Christian bookstore.

Internet: http://www.reapernet.com
Prices subject to change without notice.

D *Destiny Image*
New Releases